Raku

Chilton Book Company · Radnor, Pennsylvania

Steven Branfman

Raku

A Practical Approach

Designed by Tracy Baldwin
Photographs by Marna Kennedy unless otherwise noted
Drawings by Jodine Kuhlman unless otherwise noted
Manufactured in the United States of America

Library of Congress Cataloging in Publication Data
Branfman, Steven.
        Raku : a practical approach / Steven Branfman.
            p.   cm.
        Includes bibliographical references and index.
        Summary: Explains the history, concepts, and
    techniques for making raku pottery.
        ISBN 0-8019-8183-2—ISBN 0-8019-8023-2 (pbk.)
        1. Pottery craft.   2. Raku pottery.   [1. Pottery
    craft.   2. Raku pottery.]   I. Title.
    TT920.B72   1991
    738.1'4—dc20   90-55875
                                              CIP
                                              AC

    4 5 6 7 8 9 0   9 8 7 6

I first met Jerry DiGuisto in 1970 at Cortland State College. I was a freshman art student with little in the way of formal studio art training or understanding of what I was about to embark on. Jerry was a big fellow, intimidating in stance and professional stature, yet as I was soon to learn, friendly and—dare I say—gentle in his manner. Jerry always seemed to be the center of activity, not necessarily in a formal sense but rather in a spiritual sense, almost as a guru. The upperclass students were always around him talking art, politics, and the issues of the day. As fate would have it, I decided to major in sculpture and Jerry became my academic adviser. Over the next four years I learned more about art and the artist than I ever imagined there was to learn. As I began to be drawn to pottery, Jerry did his best to make me feel guilty about abandoning sculpture. I felt like a defector. Only later did I realize that this was his way of helping me to be sure of my decision.

A year after graduating, I returned to visit, unsure about how Jerry would react to me. In five minutes he cleaned me out of my best pots. He approved.

This book is dedicated to the memory of my professor Jerald DiGuisto. His advice, influence, and warmth opened my eyes to the value and meaning of art. His inspiration lives on in the young minds that he touched.

Contents

Foreword

Another book on raku? That was my first reaction when Steven Branfman told me he was writing *Raku: A Practical Approach*. Books on raku have been written by at least a dozen authors over the last fifteen years in the United States and abroad. In fact, I was amused last year when in the Soviet Union I was shown a book in Hungarian entitled *Raku for Children*. So it was natural for me to ask Steven to justify his book. As an explanation, he sent me the manuscript. What makes his raku book different?

For starters, it's his personal explanation of the history, concepts, and techniques for making raku. His first-person instruction sounds more like an inspired teacher than the writing of an objective reporter. The book is full of encouragement—encouragement to experiment, to question, to be curious, to accept, to understand raku in more than one dimension. Among other things, this book is a useful teaching tool. For example, the immediacy of watching glazes mature instead of watching cones drop. For some, it can be a new aesthetic, one that goes beyond our Western need for absolute control and perfection. For others, it offers the possibility of invention. It can even be financially rewarding in that copper lusters, crackle glazes, and richly smoked surfaces are highly valued for sale.

One of Steven's goals was to avoid writing a "how-to" book. To this end, he succeeds rather well. The concepts and principles he discusses can be grasped and expanded by the inquisitive mind. On the other hand, the detailed formulas and specific information he gives concerning all aspects of raku making are addressed to those who want more help.

Since 1960, American-style raku has expanded in an almost bewildering explosion of techniques, processes, and glaze formulas. As a result, the simple four-page explanation of raku I wrote in the 1960s is now complicated enough to require 170 pages! Steven's accurate historical survey, as well as his personal aesthetic and philosophical overview give his book a straightforward appeal that should be of interest to every potter.

Paul Soldner
Claremont, California

Acknowledgments

Realizing the completion of this book is the result of the combined efforts of many people, and I would like to extend my sincere thanks to all those who helped. First, to my parents, who, each in their own way, encouraged my interest and study in art, and to my high school art teacher, Pat Buzawa, who first showed me both the fun and seriousness of doing art. David Manzella helped make it possible for me to study pottery and education at the Rhode Island School of Design, and Norm Shulman (with great difficulty) awakened a sense of criticism and objectivity in me toward my own art.

Thanks go to my wife, Ellen, for her ever-present encouragement, support, and understanding, and to my sons, Jared and Adam, who, with trepidation, relinquished their computer time to me and had to do without *Brickles* and *Tetris* while I wrote this book.

I would also like to thank Carol Temkin, Jodie Kuhlman, and the entire staff at The Potters Shop and School who held down the fort in my absence while I worked on this book. I know it was unbearable. (They can't wait until I start my next book.) Special thanks to Jodie, who took time from her busy schedule to do all the wonderful drawings.

I am indebted to Marna Kennedy for her enthusiasm, patience, and long, arduous hours on location and in the darkroom, and my friends John Heller and Dan Levinson for their invaluable criticism of the manuscript. Rick Hirsch sent me a tape recounting his enlightening experience in Kyoto with the Raku Family.

A special note of thanks goes to Charles Weyerhaeuser and William Thrasher of the Art Complex Museum in Duxbury, Massachusetts. Mr. Weyerhaeuser allowed me to examine and photograph the museum's collection of traditional raku ware, and Bill Thrasher generously shared his knowledge of and experience with the Japanese tea ceremony and the raku tradition.

I owe great debt to the countless people I have encountered throughout my career. It is their generosity in sharing knowledge and experience with me and others that keeps the development and evolution of creativity alive and strengthens our individual efforts at success.

Finally, I want to thank those individuals who specifically shared photographs, recipes, experiences, techniques, advice, and general knowledge with me. Each one lives by the axiom that we can all be teachers, effective and appreciated, only if we maintain a commitment to being students of what we someday hope to be experts in.

Raku

Introduction

Those of us who work in raku are in the midst of one of the most exciting creative processes there is. Raku is happening in art schools, craft centers, elementary schools, and studios all over the country, and in fact all over the world. What makes this even more astounding is that raku has only been practiced in the West over the past thirty years. Western raku is a process that is young and as you will see, through an interesting chain of events, we have truly made our own.

A Practical Approach

When I began experimenting with raku, I read what books and articles there were, searching for the information I needed to understand *how to do raku*. I found historical and cultural accounts, explanations of the philosophical foundations, and assorted technical information, but no single source tied everything together into a nice neat package that would serve as a complete handbook. The information always seemed to go up to a certain point and no further. I know that had there been a comprehensive, easy-to-follow, step-by-step handbook, my early efforts would have been more fruitful and less frustrating.

Raku: A Practical Approach is the book that would have served me well in those earlier years, for it is a book written to be used. You won't find technical or scientific overkill or self-elevating philosophy. That has all been done elsewhere. You also won't find a how-to manual on basic pottery techniques such as hand-building, throwing, or glazing. These techniques and processes also have been explained again and again in numerous compendiums written expressly with the beginning pottery student in mind. This book assumes a basic knowledge and skill in pottery and a familiarity with basic terminology, as well as rudimentary experience with kilns. I hope you will find in this book a useful raku manual that above all will give you the confidence to build and fire a raku kiln and your pots.

My own introduction to raku came as an innocent bystander when I was a graduate student at the Rhode Island School of Design. Working quietly in my studio one day, the calm was suddenly disturbed by a student bursting through the doors of the kiln room. He was coughing and tears were streaming from his eyes as a cloud of smoke followed him through the hallway:

> "What are you doing?" I asked.
> "Raku!" He cried out through the smoke.
> "What's that?" I asked, intrigued.
> "Firing technique!"

That's all he said, but that was enough. I was curious and wanted to know more. The work from that student's firing was actually rather dull, but I still wanted to learn more. The first thing I learned was that indoors is not the ideal location for raku firing and clouds of smoke are not a prerequisite for success! But no matter what the setting or the amount of experience you bring with you, the raku process is exciting and the results are never completely predictable. I was also student teaching at the time at a local prep school and thought that through raku I might be able to interest the somewhat "less than interested in art" students in pottery. Even after being told by my pottery friends that the chances of success in building and firing a wood-fired raku kiln without having any experience with raku, or kiln building for that matter, was probably just as difficult as receiving an NEA grant, I forged ahead anyway. And my efforts were successful!

I've been doing raku ever since, and I

Author. Vase. 1988. Wheel-thrown; poured glaze. 32" h. Photo: Robert Arruda.

continue to make exciting, new discoveries. Raku is as fresh for me now as it was that day fifteen years ago when that teary-eyed student burst through the doors. I've always tried to be simple in my approach and not become too absorbed with technical details that I can find in books. I do, however, know where to look! (I'll tell you.) So be confident in your knowledge, be excited about experimenting, and above all don't be afraid to fail (I won't let you.) As my first pottery teacher, John Jessiman at Cortland State College, used to say when observing our first halting attempts to master a new process: "Don't worry. It's only clay!"

Frequently Asked Questions and Common Misconceptions about Raku

Raku is a technique that carries with it many misconceptions. Chances are that if you are reading this book you either share some of them or have some questions you would like to have answered immediately. It seems to me that a good way to start the learning process is to present the most common questions asked of me during classes, workshops, and demonstrations.

Doesn't raku mean only that you fire your pots in a pit instead of a kiln?

No, you would put your pots in a pit only if they are rubble and you're using them for landfill. Pit firing, smoke firing, and sawdust firing are often confused with raku firing, although the contemporary raku potter often uses ideas and concepts borrowed from those processes. Briefly, raku ware is fired in a more or less conventional kiln using standard glaze technology. Pit firing is a primitive technique in which the ware is loaded into a shallow pit and surrounded by fuel, usually wood. Maturing temperatures are generally lower than kiln-fired ware and glazes are not used.

Is raku also a philosophy, a religion, or a Buddhist ceremony?

Any or all of the above is true, depending on the potter.

Didn't Paul Soldner invent raku?

Raku is a Japanese pottery technique. Soldner is an innovator of that technique and one of a few responsible for popularizing raku in the United States in the 1950s and 1960s. Soldner was one of the first to use postfiring smoking as part of the raku process.

Is raku suitable for functional work?

The traditional use of raku ware in the Japanese tea ceremony has contributed to confusion about the functional use of raku. All raku-fired ware is fragile, porous, and generally unsuitable for functional use. Think of raku as *decorative*.

Why can't I get my kiln to temperature no matter how much gas I use?

Chances are that you don't have a sufficient air/gas mixture and your atmosphere is overreducing. You would need to increase your primary and secondary air sources.

Isn't raku a once-fire process where you don't have to bisque first?

No! Raku firing greenware is a sure way to line the bottom of your kiln with shards. Resist the temptation.

Which cones do I use in raku?

The only cones that should be used near a raku kiln are ice cream cones. Because of the fast firing, varying atmosphere, multiple loads, and other factors, cones are essentially useless. Raku is fired using the actual glaze melt as the visual indicator of maturity. Well, yes, I'll admit that there are some cases where cones or a pyrometer *may* be useful, such as firing a load of unglazed ware for matt and smoke effects, or when your maturing temperature is so fixed and consistent that monitoring the glaze melt is unnecessary.

What's the difference between raku and salt firing?

Salt firing and other forms of vapor glazing are sometimes confused with raku. Salt firing means introducing sodium into the kiln during the firing. You can do this at a variety of temperatures. Sodium from the salt combines with alumina and silica in the clay to form a glaze on the ware. Raku and salt firing also are often confused because vapor glazing can be used in *combination* with raku firing.

Can I fire raku in an electric kiln?

Most certainly.

Don't the tongs used to lift the pots from the kiln leave marks?

Sometimes they do. Usually, though, the glaze is still molten enough to smooth out any marks. In either case, tong marks should not be treated as defects but rather as characteristics of raku.

How do you get those bright metallic effects? Sometimes my glazes don't crackle as much as I would like them to. What can I do?

Assuming you are using the correct glazes, both metallic effects and dark crackle lines are a result of correct glaze application and a fast postfiring reduction. You must quickly remove your pot from the kiln to the reduction container and cover the container before the pot has a chance to reoxidize.

So many raku glaze recipes contain lead. Do I have to use lead to get interesting results?

While lead has been used for centuries as the preferred low-temperature flux in glazes, we now know that lead can be dangerous and working with it puts you at unnecessary risk. You do not have to use lead at all or ever again.

How much experience do I need to be able to do raku on my own? I've seen it done a few times, but it looks complicated. Can I really build my own kiln? What do I need to get started? Help!

Before you become involved in raku, you need to have a basic familiarity with pottery-making and firing techniques. You can obtain this by taking a class at a local pottery or craft center or through an adult education program. I also suggest reading a good general pottery handbook to supplement the class. Yes, you can build your own kiln. What do you need to get started? A good pottery course, a willingness to learn and to be frustrated at times, and this book. Good luck!

What is Raku?

Chapter 1

Some potters know more about what raku *is not* than about what it *is*. At its most rudimentary technical level, raku can be described as a low-fire pottery technique in which pieces are placed in a preheated kiln and brought up to temperature quickly. When the glaze has matured, the pieces are removed from the kiln with tongs and cooled immediately in water, cooled slowly in the open air, or placed in a barrel of combustible material, covered, and allowed to smoke for some predetermined amount of time.

Sounds simple enough. However, even those new to the technique probably are aware of the cultural and historical aura associated with raku that often seems inseparable to the potters who are involved with it. So where is all our history, our dedication to authentic historical technique, and our reverence of past Zen masters? The fact is that raku can be whatever you want it to be. There is no doubt that a case can be made for abandoning the word *raku* altogether in favor of a more relevant descriptive term, but when I refer to raku, it is not without a respect for its origins. With that in mind, I feel no compulsion to rename a technique simply because at present it may not embody all of its original conceptions. It may be a cliché to say that raku is different things to different people, but it is true.

Further confusion between the labeling of traditional raku and how we personalize it is illustrated through an experience as told by Rick Hirsch. In 1978 in Kyoto Rick demonstrated how raku was done in the United States and also participated in a panel discussion with Paul Soldner and the fourteenth-generation Kichizaemon. Kichizaemon, or Raku-san, is the title of the current head of the Raku Family. Not realizing that raku was known, let alone appreciated and possibly

1-1
Patrick Crabb places a 55-gallon drum over one of his large pieces during the smoking phase of the raku process.

understood, outside Japan, Raku-san was extremely impressed with this American method of firing. After observing this process for the first time, he described what he saw by calling his raku a "butterfly" and this new, Americanized modification a "bird." In his eyes, American potters had taken raku beyond its traditional boundaries. Despite the excitement he felt for this technique (postfiring reduction and fuming) and the praise he had for it, he was somewhat confused by it being called raku. During the ensuing panel discussion, Tadanari Mitsuoka, a prominent Japanese art historian, adamantly refused to recognize this process as raku, thus reaffirming Raku-san's confusion. The possibility that anyone other than the Raku Family could produce "raku" was inconceivable. At that moment, Soldner, responding to the compelling differences between raku as practiced by Raku-san and his family and "raku" as practiced by himself and other American potters, termed his ware *ukar*, or *raku* spelled backwards.

Let's begin by being true to our understanding of the concept of raku. Raku is without question a pottery technique sure and technical as cone 10 reduction, salt firing, or terra sigilatta. Each of those techniques has a historical and cultural chronicle, and so does raku. It is interesting, though, that if we want to learn salt firing, for instance, we are not compelled to feel we are being disrespectful if we don't thoroughly research the history and social context of German salt-glazed ware and its origins and development in the twelfth to fifteenth centuries. Even less important is whether or not we faithfully adhere to the aesthetic or spiritual approach to the technique. So why is the opposite true when it comes to raku?

Perhaps the most obvious reason is the name *raku* itself—that the Japanese word always reminds us of its origins. Perhaps because many of us feel that our own pottery roots emanate from Eastern civilization rather than Western, we feel a sense of guilt when we lay claim to a process that seemingly should remain solely with the Zen masters. Whatever the reason, raku does compel us to connect in some way with the past.

Raku offers us the best of two worlds. While raku is deeply rooted in Japanese tradition, its contemporary incarnation is very different. So, I can simultaneously work in a traditional technique where all

1–2
Rick Hirsch demonstrates American-style raku in Kyoto at the World's Crafts Council Conference, 1978. Yutaka Kondo, pottery teacher at Kyoto City College, explains the process to the Prince and Princess of Japan. At right is Ake Huldt, then secretary-general of the WCC. Photo: Bob Vigiletti.

the rules have been set *and* in a contemporary technique where the rules are being set as we work. While I never forget raku's origins while I work, I cannot claim to be true to the ideals of the first raku potters. My approach, like that of most contemporary potters working in raku, does not pay homage to Chojiro, Rikyu, or Ogata Kenzan, and perhaps for this reason alone I should not call what I do "raku." But so long as I appreciate and respect the origins of raku, why should I call it something else?

Another attitude regarding the mean-

1–3
Raku Tan'nyu (1795–1854). Red raku tea bowl.
3¼" h × 4¼" w. The storage box, inscribed "Red tea
bowl," has the raku seal and is signed by Raku
Tan'nyu, the tenth-generation Kichizaemon. This
bowl is rich with carbon deposits. Collection of the
Art Complex Museum, Duxbury, Massachusetts.

ing of raku involves us in what is perhaps the most fundamental and philosophical approach of all. Paul Soldner writes of a "rakuness" that we can strive for that transcends any one pottery-making technique, or in fact any individual kind of creative act. As potters we realize our creativity through stoneware, porcelain, or sculpture, and, yes, through "raku." It is a *state* of achievement attainable through a perceived effortlessness that has no ties to any one form of expression, culture, or religion. Perhaps that is the true meaning of raku.

In a contemporary, technical context, we describe raku as the *firing* process be-

1–4
Author. Vase. 1988. Wheel-
thrown, poured glaze. 14" h.
Photo: Robert Arruda.

cause firing is what clearly differentiates raku from other pottery techniques. Most firing processes involve loading the ware into a cold kiln, firing slowly, and through the use of pyrometric cones determining the maturing point of the glaze, then turning off the kiln and allowing it to cool before removing the ware. Conventional firing and cooling may take anywhere from 24 to 48 hours or longer. Another difference between raku ware and conventional pottery is that raku ware is fragile because of the heat shock forced upon the clay. The heat shock, combined with the chemical makeup of the clay and glaze, also renders the ware porous and soft. The work is not waterproof, and because the glazes universally craze (a desirable effect), raku ware cannot be used for serving food. The bacteria from food would become absorbed into the crazed areas with prolonged use. Vigorous cleaning would eventually cause the work to self-destruct! Therefore, raku should be seen as decorative, not functional.

When we make conventional pottery, we know that once the piece is glazed and put into the kiln the creative part is finished, except of course for a skillful firing. Raku firing, however, extends our creative involvement as far into the process as we care to go. Our eyes are always on the piece, judging, determining, deciding, and altering. We end the firing when we see fit, without the aid of cones or other temperature-measuring devices. We alone determine the next steps. In addition, the rules or conventions in raku change as your expectations change.

By now you see that certain basic requirements must be met in order to do raku in any of its forms. These requirements involve both an intellectual and a technical understanding, as well as the practical considerations of having the right equipment, tools, supplies, and space. We

1–5
Marvin Sweet. Aditya No. 7. *1990. Combination of thrown and hand-built forms. 21" × 9" × 9". Photo: Charle Mayer.*

must use a clay body that will withstand rapid heating and cooling. When forming a piece, we must keep in mind the kind of physical torture they must be able to withstand throughout the firing. Glazes must be suitable in maturing temperature. Kilns must be designed to allow for rapid temperature increase and to accommodate the quick removal of the ware. In addition, the kiln must be set up in an appropriate place. Raku is usually more than a one-person process, so you must have helpers to facilitate the firing.

1–6
Dennis Parks. Epigraphic
Fragment: OF TRUST.
*1983. 12″ × 17″. This piece
was fired face down on a
piece of plywood, impregnat-
ing the clay with carbon deposits. Courtesy the artist.*

As we proceed in our study of the raku technique, you will see how you can meet all these requirements. If you take the time to learn the rationale behind the process, you will obtain the confidence and knowledge to try raku on your own. As you learn the general techniques, don't become locked into another person's aesthetic or even quality assessment. Use the raku process to make your own statement.

Raku: A Brief Historical and Philosophical Perspective

Chapter 2

As modern potters interested in pursuing a contemporary process, why should we consider the origins and historical significance of raku? There are those who maintain that the only real raku is that which is done for the traditional Japanese tea ceremony, using traditional techniques in order to obtain spiritual harmony. Others regard raku simply as an enjoyable hobby. But for many, myself included, raku is a creative pottery technique with undeniable connections to a rich spiritual and cultural heritage where there is still much to be discovered, experienced, and shared.

At his workshops, Makoto Yabe, a Japanese potter friend, often tells of his apprenticeship in Japan. He explains matter of factly how he spent the first six months just sweeping up after the master. Then he spent the next six months learning how to wedge, to center, and so on. As if on cue, the faces of the participants drop and some go as far as to ask why he stood for that kind of treatment. "To learn," Makoto explains, "to learn." Although to some it may seem mundane, perhaps that is the answer: simply to learn.

The Role of Tradition

As a craftsperson, you are part of a history and a tradition, part of an evolution in a chain of education and experience that you may add to as you master the craft. Taking the fastest path is not always the best. The goal of learning anything new should be to amass an inventory of knowledge that can be applied in whole or in part to solving a particular problem. In this case, an aesthetic one. Developing a historical perspective places us in a time frame, allowing us not only to appreciate the efforts of our predecessors but also to learn from them. At the same time, we learn how to be innovative.

The Western evolution of raku and our present-day practice of it has led some potters to advocate a differentiation between the two techniques. I contend, however, that calling our version of raku by its Japanese name allows us to connect intellectually and philosophically with its spiritual beginnings. Our practice of raku, even with our Western innovations and aesthetic principles, is still intimately connected to the spirit and traditional practice of the original technique.

The story of how raku evolved from a Japanese ritual to a wealth of contemporary settings is an interesting one. We know that raku as a style of pottery originated in Kyoto in the late sixteenth century with the potter Chojiro, a Korean immigrant. Bernard Leach in *A Potter's Book* tells us that Chojiro's parents, Ameya and Teirin, were the first to produce ware of the type we associate with raku, but it was Chojiro, under the guidance and tutelage of the great Kyoto tea master Sen-no-Rikyu, who brought the ware to the attention of the emperor Hideyoshi. Hideyoshi, in memory of Chojiro, bestowed a gold seal on Chojiro's son Jokei. The word *raku* comes from the ideograph engraved on that gold seal. Loosely translated, it can mean enjoyment, pleasure, comfort, happiness, or contentment.

Raku was prized by Japanese tea masters because it is unpretentious but aesthetically pleasing and embodies the ideals of Zen Buddhism and *wabi*. In Japanese aesthetics, *wabi* encompasses austerity, transcience, seclusion, and tranquillity. *Wabi* is the intangible essence of the tea ceremony. On the practical side, the porous clay body acts as insulation between

2–1
Attributed to Raku Chonyu (1714–69), the seventh-generation Kichizaemon. Tea Bowl. 3" h × 3¾" w. This bowl is characterized by a wonderfully leather-like texture and dark brown glaze interrupted by a red cloud-like area. Collection of the Art Complex Museum, Duxbury, Massachusetts.

the hot tea and the hand and produces a dull, quiet sound when it comes in contact with utensils or the table top.

It is difficult to know exactly the details involved in the raku firing process in Chojiro's time, but we can assume that the ware was placed in a preheated kiln, quickly brought up to temperature, removed from the kiln with some kind of tongs, and allowed to cool in the air. Just how this method of firing developed is also a matter of speculation. One story is that in an effort to speed up the firing process in the production of roof tiles, impatient potters removed the tiles from the kiln with tongs. Much to their surprise, the tiles remained intact despite the rapid cooling. In fact, Chojiro was a maker of roof tiles, and the earliest existing example of his work is thought to have been fired in this way.

Traditional raku falls broadly into two categories: red raku and black raku. Red raku is made with a red earthenware clay, glazed with a creamy clear glaze, fired quickly to a low temperature, and removed from the kiln and allowed to cool. (See color Plates 1 and 2.) Some sources state that the red color is achieved by covering the clay with an ochre slip prior to glazing. Black raku, on the other hand, is made with a stoneware clay, decorated with a black glaze, and fired higher, probably to stoneware temperatures. Firing is slower, with rapid cooling contributing to the black color and the texture of the ware. Some sources have assumed that raku ware is fired without a bisque firing, but this is not true. All of the research indicates that a normal bisque firing was done prior to the raku firing.

Raku was first brought to the attention of the Western world by Bernard Leach, a painter who had no experience with pottery. In 1911, while living in Japan, he attended the same kind of "raku party" that introduced many of us to raku. He describes potters decorating bisque ware with strange pigments and dipping them in a thick glaze prior to placing the pots in a preheated kiln. Much to Leach's surprise, the pots did not break, and after half an hour or so they were removed from the kiln and allowed to cool. He was amazed that the pots did not break under the high temperatures in the kiln and the rapid cooling.

Needless to say, it was this experience with raku that inspired Leach to study pottery. For Leach, raku was a jumping-off point. He viewed raku as a way to have fun with pottery, a way to entertain his friends and customers, but as a pottery technique he felt it had limited creative possibilities for a contemporary studio potter who wanted to develop a personal style and make an artistic statement through clay. A common misconception, probably contributed to by Leach's account of his first raku experience, is that the raku firing is part of the Japanese tea ceremony. This of course is not true.

Warren Gilbertson was probably the first potter to introduce raku to the United States directly. He was living and working in Japan in 1938–40 and upon his return to the States the Art Institute of Chicago held a major exhibition of his work. While no written account of the show exists today, it seems certain that some raku pieces were among the several hundred pieces exhibited. In 1942 Gilbertson presented a paper at the annual meeting of the American Ceramic Society in which he described the raku process, glazes, decoration, and types of kilns. Interestingly enough, he makes only a cursory comment regarding any cultural significance that raku may have had. He viewed the technique as a curiosity that could be used to introduce pottery making to beginners! Gilbertson was at the forefront of the newly emerging American contemporary studio pottery movement. Tragically, he died in an auto crash in 1954 before the movement was fully under way.

The beginning of raku in America beyond Gilbertson's introduction of the technique are difficult to ascertain. The potter who is responsible for establishing raku as a popular, creative method of pottery making is Paul Soldner. Soldner began his raku experiments around 1960 with only the information gathered from Leach in *A Potter's Book*. Being somewhat bored and dissatisfied with the apparent bland nature of the color development in the pots, Soldner spontaneously put a piece in some leaves to burn. Thus was born our con-

2–2
Paul Soldner. Sculptured Vessel. *1989. Wheel-thrown and altered with copper slip; low-fire salt fumed. 23" h × 32" w × 8" d. Collection of Saugre De Christo Museum, Pueblo, Colorado. Courtesy the artist.*

temporary incarnation of the raku process—"postfiring reduction."

Soldner has been at the forefront of raku from those earliest days. As his influence spread, so did the popularity of raku. Hal Riegger, another early pioneer in the American raku movement, began with and maintained a steadfast commitment to a more traditional and spiritual involvement with raku. Riegger advocated the use of wood- and coal-burning kilns, as well as making raku ware using standard hand-building methods. He presented workshops and demonstrations and in 1958 taught raku at the Haystack Mountain School of Crafts. Unknown to each other, Riegger and Soldner were experimenting with raku at the same time. Riegger also developed the American method of postfiring reduction. Although Riegger began to experiment with raku in 1948, twelve years before Soldner, it was perhaps because of his quiet, reserved approach to working that he has never been fully credited with this innovation.

2–3
Hal Riegger. Tea Bowl. *Pinched and carved heavily grogged clay; thick semiwhite glaze. Courtesy the artist.*

2–4
Jean Griffith. Raku Vase. *1962. Slab-built vessel with thrown and altered additions. 14" h. The simple lead glaze was adapted from Bernard Leach's* A Potter's Book. *Photo: Don Normark.*

About the same time, Jean Griffith and some fellow graduate students at the University of Washington were experimenting with the raku process. Using Leach as a guide as well, they held raku parties and presented demonstrations. They too included a postfiring reduction phase as part of the technique, but as Jean relates, they did not know whose idea it was! Raku was truly in its infancy. In fact, when Soldner held a workshop in Seattle in 1962, there was no mention of raku. Sold-

ner, Riegger, Griffith, and the others were truly breaking new creative ground. They had no experts to guide them and no one to answer their questions. Their experiments were simply carried out through trial and error and they tried to make their accidents work aesthetically. Not until Soldner visited Japan in the early 1970s did it become clear to him that the process of smoking the ware was not part of the traditional practice of raku. The Japanese

2–5
Susan and Steven Kemenyffy. The Ending. *Side 2. 1989. Raku sculpture. 48" × 24" × 8". Hand-built and incised; commercial glazes fired to cone 5½ and reduced in a pit with cardboard. Photo: MMG Photography.*

raku potters told him that he was involved in a process all his own.

Raku is most certainly still evolving. Having begun on the West Coast, it has moved past the "raku mania" of the 1970s and 1980s, when it had fad-like appeal. Raku now exists coast to coast, ocean to ocean, and seems to have settled into a mainstream process. Keep in mind, though, that as the American form of raku continues to expand and develop, the fifteenth generation of the Raku Family is producing traditional raku tea ware in Japan unaffected by its contemporary coun-

terpart. Other leaders in the development of the raku technique include Wayne Higby, David Middlebrook, Angelo Garzio, Jim Romberg, Rick Hirsch, and Susan and Steven Kemenyffy, who, along with others, have contributed stimulating perspectives and notable variations to this exciting process.

The Aesthetics of Raku

Any discussion of the aesthetics of raku must consider Zen and the Japanese tea ceremony. The tea ceremony, *Cha-no-yu*, is a formalized ritual that was established centuries ago and has been refined through the ages. Its practice is designed to invoke a uniform aesthetic response emanating from the strict preparation and drinking of tea. Central to the aesthetic of the tea ceremony are the concepts of *wabi* and *shibui*. *Wabi* is intangible, and as Yanagi explains, "its full comprehension by all people would be asking too much." *Shibui* encompasses the same attributes as *wabi*, but in a concrete way. Shibui is the visible beauty in objects, in fact the *ultimate* beauty. The tea ceremony offers us much in the way of knowledge and understanding of a culture very different from ours. I encourage you to learn more about it.

Just as a grasp of the Japanese tea ceremony is important to our understanding of raku aesthetics, so are the aesthetic boundaries that we may find ourselves a part of today. Here we need to consider raku aesthetics in relation to the position pottery as a craft has held throughout history as well as its place in contemporary society and the art world. Pottery as a distinct, descriptive term today has become blurred. No longer can we hear the word *pottery* and confidently conjure up an accurate image. Pottery is vessels, sculpture,

2–6

Author. Vase. 1989. Wheel-thrown; coil-and-throw method; poured and sponged glaze. 32" h. Photo: Robert Arruda.

2–7
Rick Hirsch. Ceremonial Cup #30. *1984–85. Thrown and hand-built; low-fire glazes sandblasted after firing. 14½" h × 14" w. Photo: Dean Powell.*

vessel-like sculpture, or essentially *anything* made of clay. Likewise, the label "potter" no longer automatically refers to the person sitting at their wheel turning functional ware. We now refer to ourselves as ceramists, clayworkers, and ceramic sculptors as well as potters. We are craftspeople, artists, artist-potters, and art-ist-craftsmen. Aesthetic concepts also have been broadened and redefined, in fact to a point that has polarized the ceramics community.

As we know, pottery has its origins in functional ware, where efforts toward function and beauty were one in the same. The potter of the day infused all of his or

2–8
Exterior/interior of Shofuan *(Pine Wind Hut) on the grounds of the Art Complex Museum. Tea host and guest at the beginning of a tea ceremony. 1989. Courtesy the Art Complex Museum, Duxbury, Massachusetts.*

her creative energies into the object without regard for that object's intended audience or use. Certainly throughout history there has also been ceremonial or other specialized ware produced for a limited audience out of the mainstream of society. For either audience, though, the intended function of a pot did not detract from our appreciation of it as an aesthetic object. This is no longer the case. Today, more and more potters find it necessary and even advantageous to their careers to abandon any semblance of function in their work. This is unfortunate, for it further separates us from the ancestry of our activity.

Cries are heard in the crafts world for a return to the production of more functional handmade objects for everyday use. It would indeed be a gentler place if handmade objects were more a part of today's households. Soetsu Yanagi, in his book *The Unknown Craftsman*, attempts to bridge the gap between Eastern and Western aesthetics with a more universal attitude toward beauty and the presence of handmade objects:

> On reflection, one must conclude that in bringing cheap and useful goods to the average household, industrialism has been of service to mankind—but at the cost of the heart, of warmth, friendliness, and beauty. By contrast, articles well made by hand, though expensive, can be enjoyed in homes for generations, and, this considered, they are not expensive after all.

Now I am not advocating the boycott of all work that is not designed to go into the dishwasher! My own work is certainly not functional in the sense of everyday use. But some handmade articles should exist solely to please the viewer. Two forces act upon my own aesthetic sensibilities: the desire to surround myself with handmade objects that I can hold and use and to sur-

2–9
Author. Vase. 1989. Wheel-thrown, coil-and-throw method; poured and sponged glaze; raku vapor-fired. 30″ h. Photo: Robert Arruda.

round myself with objects that are simply beautiful to look at. All of the creative arts should be embraced and made more integral to our lives, whether functional or nonfunctional, whether craft or fine art. At the same time, the rhetoric that encourages the polarization between different approaches and philosophies should be abandoned.

How does raku fit into this complicated picture? For me, it connects the past with the present. Raku ware was prized because of its humble, spontaneous appearance, and the innocent, uncontrived connection that it fostered between human beings and nature. It is subtle and difficult to describe, yet when we observe first-hand a raku tea bowl of the seventeenth or eighteenth century, our understanding and appreciation becomes intense and moving.

It is often said, and I agree, that there are no new ideas, only new technology and yet-undiscovered *combinations of ideas* that by themselves and in their melding have been used time and time again. An artist does not create in a vacuum. Basic to the creative process is the interaction and sharing with others; observing the world around us and being alert to the vastness of our immediate surroundings. Today, we are less likely to be driven by the ideals of Zen and more likely to be influenced by homelessness, the environment, and world peace. These feelings about our existence may or may not manifest themselves directly in our work, but undoubtedly they play a role in our perception and analysis of the qualilty of form, line, and space, which are all-important in any artistic endeavor.

The raku process may place you in unfamiliar territory. Ware that has been successful for you in the past may suddenly prove uneventful. Glaze applications, brush strokes, and textures that formerly resulted in strong statements of color and design may prove weak and feeble. Likewise, subtle effects obtained through well-practiced techniques may appear crude and uncontrolled, or they may not appear at all. You must go through a period of adjustment when exploring any new, unfamiliar area. But I encourage you to persevere until you come to grips with the raku technique and its idiosyncrasies. Embrace the aesthetic tenets even though they may seem difficult to understand at first. The more work you produce, the finer your control will become. More and more nuances of method will make themselves apparent to you. Successful work comes from a combination of technical comfort and aesthetic sophistication where neither is sacrificed in favor of the other.

We must realize that our practice of raku with all of its Western innovations and aesthetic principles has not, and will never, supersede the original spirit and traditional practice of raku. Our practice must stand alone aesthetically and not compete with its connection to the past. You may find, as I have, that raku allows you a wonderful combination of exciting technique and satisfying aesthetics, contemporary style as well as a rich historical tradition.

Clay, Pottery Forming, Glazes, and Decoration

Chapter 3

Clays

It makes sense to begin our study of the raku technique with an understanding of the appropriate types of clay bodies suitable for raku because in the absence of a clay that can withstand the process we may as well forget about the rest! First, let me debunk two myths: that one must use *raku* clay for raku firing, and that, since raku is a low-temperature technique, the clay must be a low-fire clay. Not true in either case. First of all, what is this mysterious *raku* clay? All a raku clay means is one that will fire and cool rather quickly without breaking, one that will be compatible with the glazes we wish to use, and one that will give us the required aesthetic result. These are the same considerations we apply in finding a suitable clay for *any* firing range or technique. While *almost any clay can be raku fired*, we want to use a clay that will give us the most consistent successful results—in other words, less breakage! To achieve this, choose a clay with the following characteristics:

1. An open, porous structure that does not vitrify at either the bisque or raku firing temperature.
2. A structure that has the right plasticity for the type of forming (throwing, hand-building) you will be doing.
3. The lightest color that you want to be able to achieve on your pots. For example, if you want to have white areas on your pots, choosing a red or buff clay will make your job difficult.

An open, porous structure is achieved through the liberal use of grog, silica sand, stoneware clay, or fillers such as sawdust or beach sand mixed or wedged into the clay body. Essentially, any type of commercially available stoneware clay body is suitable for raku, providing that it is not too dense and that it contains the other characteristics you wish. If you are formulating your own clay bodies, start with a stoneware clay that you have been using and simply try it, unaltered, in raku. If you think it may be too dense, wedge about 10 percent medium grog into the body. Other common materials found in raku clays are the ones you would normally associate with stoneware bodies. These include spodumene, talc, flint, feldspar, and fireclay. When using fireclay, you will have to add ball clay and small (1%) amounts of bentonite or macaloid to improve the overall plasticity of the body.

The color of the body is a matter of personal taste. I prefer a white body upon which glazes can be their brightest and offer the most contrast. No value judgment here—it's your call. Unless you add an ingredient with a high iron content or one that contains other impurities, such as Cedar Heights Redart, Jordan Clay, Calvert Clay, garden dirt (no kidding), or some other stuff you find in your studio, your clay will be mostly tan or buff to white. The purer your materials, the whiter the clay body.

What follows is a sample of clay bodies suitable for raku that I have collected over the years from various sources. The firing range (vitrification) is included for some of the clays, but this is for your information only and should not be confused with whether or not a clay is suitable for raku firing. With the exception of clay bodies high in talc, most of the clays are cone 6–10 bodies as a result of the materials (fireclay and stoneware clay) used. I have tried to give credit where the originator is known; United Kingdom equivalents are provided in brackets.

Grey Throwing Δ6–10

A.P. Green fireclay [Potclays fireclay 1275/3]	35
Cedar Heights Goldart [Potclays buff stoneware]	40
Tennessee ball clay [HVAR ball clay]	20
Custer feldspar [potash feldspar]	4
Grog	10

An excellent throwing body that is also suitable for salt firing. From John Jessiman, my first pottery teacher.

Raku #1

A.P. Green fireclay [Potclays fireclay 1275/3]	100
Cedar Heights Goldart [Potclays buff stoneware]	100
Talc	20
Bentonite	4

Soldner Raku

A.P. Green fireclay [Potclays fireclay 1275/3]	100
Tennessee ball clay [HVAR ball clay]	30
Talc	30
Grog	10

A well-known recipe from Paul Soldner. Very tough to throw.

RISD Raku Δ10

A.P. Green fireclay [Potclays fireclay 1275/3]	50
Cedar Heights Goldart [Potclays buff stoneware]	150

Custer feldspar	10
[potash feldspar]	
Grog	15

From my student days at the Rhode Island School of Design.

Higby White Raku Clay

Missouri fireclay	100 lb.
OM 4 ball clay	30 lb.
[AT ball clay]	
Talc	30 lb.
Silica sand	1%
Bisque cone 08–05	

Higby Red Raku Clay

PBX Fireclay [Potclays fireclay #6]	50 lb.
Goldart [Potclays buff stoneware]	20 lb.
Redart [Fremington clay; or add 15% potash feldspar to Etruria Marl]	25 lb.
Talc	5 lb.
Silica sand	10 lb.
Macaloid	1%
Bisque cone 08–06	

Kemenyffy Raku

Virginia Kyanite 35 mesh	30
Goldart [Potclays buff stoneware]	33
Frederick fireclay	33
Bisque cone 06	

Steven Kemenyffy developed this clay body after much research and trial and error. The use of kyanite as opposed to silica sand or grog is what allows Steven and Susan to create such massive sculptures with little breakage.

Now, how about the rumors you have heard about raku firing *porcelain*? It's true. I meant it when I said that almost any clay can be raku fired. Porcelain can be fired as well, but it requires slow and careful heating and cooling. Your success will be

3–1
Annette McCormick. Elephant Requiem. 1990. Hand-built porcelain, raku fired. 27" h × 9½" × 9½". Because of the size, some sections are fired individually and epoxied together afterward. Courtesy the artist.

greatly diminished if you try to preheat your pots and place them in a hot kiln as opposed to firing slowly from a cold kiln. You may ask yourself, Why bother trying to use porcelain in raku firing anyway? And you have a point. However, to be fair, if the whitest, smoothest, most elegant surface is your objective, then porcelain may be the way to go. If you are producing small pieces or jewelry, porcelain poses even fewer difficulties. As an alternative to using porcelain as your clay body, you may apply a layer of porcelain

3–2
Kathi Tighe. Ocarina Necklaces. *Hand-built porcelain. Photo: Tom Lange.*

slip to the surface of your piece. This will often yield the kind of whiteness you want to achieve without having to deal with the uncertainties involved in raku firing a porcelain body. Complete techniques for the successful firing of porcelain, as well as other clays, are covered in depth in Chapter 6.

Pottery-Forming Techniques

A reminder: This is not a book on beginning (or advanced, for that matter) pottery making. Many good books are available on hand-building, throwing, and sculpture as well as other clay-working techniques. Nor is this a book on general pottery for the student. Many of those are available, too. (See the Bibliography for my recommendations.) This book is for the person with a certain degree of pottery experience who wants to expand into the raku technique. The terminology used assumes a basic level of experience. Thus the discussion will be limited to how each of the following techniques is suited to the demands of the raku process and what adjustments you may need to make in your clay-forming techniques.

As in any approach to pottery making, there are three principle techniques of forming the clay into objects; hand-building, throwing, and using molds, either by slip casting, pressing, draping, or any other method.

Hand-Building

Traditional raku ware was hand-built with a deliberate, uncontrived attempt at producing a piece that looked natural, unassuming, spontaneous, and humble. This aesthetic is not akin to European standards and as such is often difficult for Westerners to incorporate into their own sensibilities. Pinching was probably the most widely used method for the making of teabowls, while it seems clear that dishes and other objects were slab-built. Warren Gilbertson, in his account of observing raku production in Japan, states that teabowls were coil-built. (And I would not necessarily assume that a potter

3-3
Raku Konyu (1857–1932). Winter tea bowl named Snowy Peak. 4¼" h × 3⅞" w. An early twentieth-century black raku bowl by the twelfth-generation Kichizaemon. A white strip of feldspar breaks up the brown to black surface. Collection of the Art Complex Museum, Duxbury, Massachusetts.

never took a stab at raku firing a piece thrown on the wheel.) During and after forming, the work was carved with simple bamboo tools.

In our context, hand-building is a perfectly acceptable method to use. Keeping in mind that any ware we wish to raku fire must be able to withstand the unkind amount of stress put on the work by the firing, hand-built pots made out of coils, slabs, or any combination of applied clay must be built with skill. Care must be taken to score and slip all joints so as to make strong bonds that will not be susceptible to expansion and separation during the firing.

Now here you are with a perfect bisque-fired load of coil pots. You glaze them, put them in the raku kiln, and

watch with horror as your coils part like an accordion on the inhale. The moral of the story is that bisque firing is not raku firing. A pot we ordinarily fire without any problems in a conventional firing may not survive the rigors of a raku. So always score and slip well to ensure a good joining of the clay. Appendages such as handles, spouts, or any protruding elements of your piece also should be attached well. In addition, consider the practicality of these elements and the likelihood of their inadvertent destruction during any part of the raku process: removing the piece from

3-4
Jodie Kuhlman. Vase. Hand-built. 26" h × 8" w. The black portion of this piece is unglazed and derives its tones from the postfiring reduction.

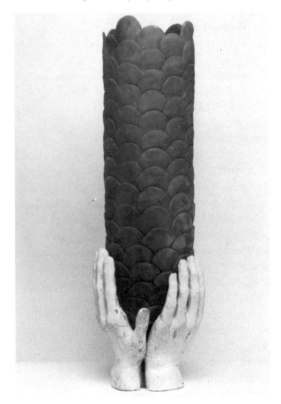

the kiln, placing the piece in the reduction container, or cleaning the piece after cooling. Don't hestitate to hand-build—just anticipate the problems, think a few steps ahead, and treat the pieces with care.

Throwing

Most contemporary pottery is thrown. The fact that traditional raku was hand-built doesn't have to condemn those of us who throw for a living to a life of scoring and slipping. Of course thrown ware is perfectly fine for raku firing. Our concerns regarding thrown pieces center around even expansion and contraction during the heating and cooling cycles. Clay should be well wedged so as to make it compact, dense, and free of lumps and air bubbles. Let me debunk another pottery misconception: pots do not crack and explode because of air bubbles. Cracking usually can be traced to clay that was still wet when fired. We want our raku clay to be bubble-free to ensure even heating and cooling. Ware should be even in wall thickness and thrown perhaps a little on the thick side rather than the thin side. Wide-bottomed forms, particularly platters, are a constant source of headaches for raku potters. Bottoms should be compressed well during the throwing process and then trimmed evenly, not leaving the clay too thick. If you are working with specialized techniques such as coil and throw, adding multiple thrown sections together, or attaching handles, spouts, or other appendages, refer to the discussion of hand-building techniques. Other than these few areas of concern, throwing poses no particular or significant problems. In fact, throwing is the safest of all the pottery-forming techniques for raku because the ware is generally made of one piece of clay that is well prepared.

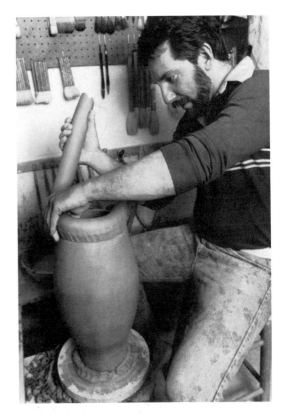

3–5
The author attaching a coil on a previously thrown, leatherhard form during the coil-and-throw technique.

Molded and Slipcast Ware

Molds can be put into two categories: molds for use with conventional clay, such as press molds and drape molds, and molds for slip casting. The former pose no particular pitfalls; the previous discussion of hand-building and throwing applies. Slip casting, however, is another ball game. The potential danger here is that slip for casting often is fine—that is, smooth, dense, nonporous, and generally non-raku-like. The slip-cast *form* is not the issue; it is the makeup of the slip used to make the form. If you can formulate a slip

3–6
Harriet Brisson. Cast Porcelain Box. *1990. Commercial and homemade glazes over masking-tape resist. 6″ × 6″ × 6″. Courtesy the artist.*

that will withstand the raku torture, then you are all set. Remember, though, that most clays (even porcelain) can be successfully raku fired if done patiently and carefully.

In summary, any method of forming ware is suitable for raku firing. Each method contains potential hazards that are avoidable if you understand the process and follow simple, logical rules as you make your pots.

Bisque Firing

It is appropriate to discuss bisque firing as we end our discussion of clays, thus keeping it separate from the raku firing itself. Bisque firing presents another area of disagreement among practitioners of raku. Some potters contend that ware should be bisqued anywhere from 1 to 3 cones lower than the conventional bisque firing. Others insist that the work has a much higher

rate of survival if it is fired 1 to 3 cones higher. Others advocate a normal bisque firing, while still others do not bisque fire at all. So where do I stand? *Definitely bisque your ware prior to raku firing.*

The raku technique is not a once-fire or raw glazing process. The purpose of bisque firing is to render the ware somewhat stronger so that you can handle it safely during glazing and kiln loading. And in the case of raku, you want to render the clay more resistant to heat shock. Bisque ware generally will absorb a safe amount of glaze and will not be weakened as it is wet by the glaze application.

My current raku clay is a commercial cone 9 stoneware clay body that I bisque to cone 08. This body gives me consistently successful results in the raku firing. Here is the logic: If you bisque too low, the clay may be too absorbent, soak up too much glaze, and either crack in the firing or give you undesirable glaze results. Under-bisque firing may also render the clay too fragile to allow for glazing at all. Bisque firing too high may make the clay too dense, nonporous, and too close to vitrification, causing cracking as a result of the clay's inability to expand and contract quickly enough.

If you don't bisque at all? Well, you open yourself up to all kinds of unnecessary dangers and disasters. For one thing, greenware would have to be raku fired considerably more slowly and would be much more prone to cracking while you tried to preheat your next load on top of the kiln. Both factors would detract from one of the main attractions of the raku process—speed and spontaneity. To be fair, though, some potters maintain that greenware is more susceptible to the effects of atmospheric changes and smoking than bisque ware. Having painstakingly raku fired greenware on several occasions and not having recognized any differences in the final results (save for my nerves), I repeat my original advice: bisque your ware prior to raku firing.

Yet another approach is the wet-firing raku technique. Not only is bisque firing rendered obsolete, but drying is done away with altogether. The theory behind wet firing is that the piece is surrounded by an envelope of steam, thereby creating an equilibrium of pressure that will prevent cracking. Frankly, I see no reason for it. For the wet-firing technique to work, the piece must be fresh off the wheel—no time for trimming. A hand-built pot would be too dry by the time you were finished. Loading a wet, soft piece into the kiln successfully would be a feat in itself. Basically you would no longer be in the realm of raku—you would be into something else altogether!

Should you bisque in an electric or fuel-burning kiln? Do whatever is easier and more convenient. It makes no difference in the end result. As far as what cone you should bisque to, if you are using a commercial clay body, bisque to the recommended cone. If you are using your own clay body and are trying raku for the first time, bisque as you have been doing. If you are using one of the clay body recipes given earlier in the chapter, bisque to cone 08 over a seven- or eight-hour cycle (depending on the size and thickness of your pots—longer for bigger and thicker) unless otherwise noted.

Glazes, Slips, and Color

Ah, you say, here come the secrets of the raku masters—those beautiful coppers, purples, and iridescent effects. Forget it, maybe later. First the basics.

Raku is a low-fire technique. No, you did not get me on a technicality. I know that I said traditional black raku is fired to stoneware temperatures, but in practice I am limiting raku to a low-fire process. Now, what is low fire for some may not be low fire for others. Raku is fired in the cone 011–06 range. I fire my work in the cone 09–07 range. You may certainly stray from this range if you wish. You must, however, decide on a firing range, formulate your glazes, and stay within that range. If you are using glazes with varying maturing temperatures that are out of the range of each other, you will not be able to achieve uniform melting on your piece. Just as cumbersome is a kiln loaded to the brim with some perfectly mature pieces while others are barely melting. In this case, some pots will have to be sacrificed to the kiln gods for the sake of the others.

As you hone in on your desired glazes, keep in mind that a maturing range of 2, 3, or 4 cones is not unusual in the low temperatures of raku, and a wider range certainly will give you more latitude. However, unless you plan to load and fire the kiln knowing that you are going to have to pull pots out at different times as their respective glazes mature, be sure to stay within an acceptable firing range. You want to avoid being caught in the predicament of having to "underfire" or "overfire" some work in order to have another piece come out "right." Flexibility to control the maturing of all of your glazes simultaneously is a worthy goal!

So what is a raku glaze? Any glaze that will give you your desired effects in the raku firing process. Because raku glazes need not conform to the same high technical standards that, for instance, glazes used for functional ware must attain, they tend to be simple in composition. Results that would ordinarily be categorized as defects not only can be perfectly acceptable in raku but often are the desired result. Crazing, or crackling, is a common example of a poor-glaze–clay-body fit that would be unacceptable for functional ware but is desirable (and often uncontrollable) in raku. Crawling, characterized by bare areas on the ware after firing that were previously glazed, is another, and there are more depending on your aesthetic.

As we begin to discuss glaze recipes, you will find a conspicuously missing low-fire glaze material, that four-letter word—*lead*. My opinion is a simple one: Why expose yourself to a danger that is avoidable? Although traditional raku glazes and, for that matter, many low-fire glazes in general use lead as the basic flux, I don't see any reason to use lead in my work. Pottery is a craft laden with dangers and risks as it is. And if we look at lead from an aesthetic point of view, we find that lead-based glazes do not work well in reducing atmospheres, especially the atmospheres that one encounters in the raku process. Reduction often causes bubbly, muddy, and gun-metal-type surfaces and does not foster the development of the kind of deep, rich, sometimes metallic and lustrous effects that are obtainable by using alkaline glazes. This is not to say that pleasing, intriguing surfaces are not possible using lead. Of course they are, as attested to by the myriad lead-based raku glazes floating around in books, glaze notes, and on people's pots. In fact, lead-based glazes do offer some advantages, such as a high index of refraction resulting in more brilliant surfaces, low surface tension, giving the glaze the ability to smooth out and cover potential defects, and a wide firing range. I contend, though, that even taking all of this into consideration, using lead exposes you to an unnecessary risk.

Arriving at a desirable selection of glazes begins with rather simple recipes that by themselves would give us basic clear glazes. Using these base recipes, you can begin to experiment with any number of oxides, stains, salts, and opacifiers on your own. You can certainly alter these or any other recipes by making simple additions or subtractions. For a slightly lower firing glaze, add a bit more flux or substitute a lower melting flux such as borax, or add a bit more clay to raise the maturing temperature. The point is, you do not need a great knowledge of glaze formula-

3–7

Kathi Tighe. Triple-Chambered Ocarina. *Thrown and hand-built. 8" h × 7½" × 7½". Photo: Dean Powell.*

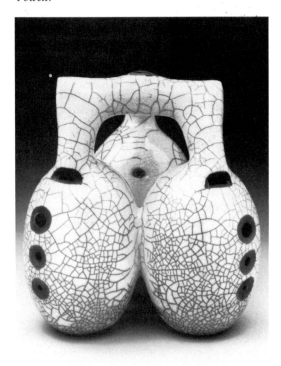

3–8
Steven and Bonnie Barisof.
Vase and Bowl. *1987.
Vase, 7¾" h × 6½" w. Bowl,
5" h × 8½" w. Stoneware
clay, raku fired and reduced
in newspaper. Their designs
are carved into the leatherhard clay with a pencil.
Glaze application is with
small brushes, being careful
to avoid the carved lines and
other areas meant to be unglazed. Courtesy the artists.*

tion or chemistry to come up with success-ful glazes of your own, so long as you do not stray too much from the base glaze.

All the standard coloring oxides are fair game for experimentation. For various luster effects, try different combinations of copper (either carbonate or oxide) with co-balt, manganese, or iron. When using co-balt, a sneeze full ($\frac{1}{4}$–$\frac{1}{2}$%) is usually enough to give you a blue with enough presence. Copper can be used in amounts up to 5 percent and more, although 2 percent will usually do the trick. Iron, manganese, nickel, and rutile are effective in amounts as little as 1 percent. Chrome is a rather strong colorant in raku and should be tried in small ($\frac{1}{2}$–1%) amounts. Keep in mind, though, that lusters of copper and silver so sought after during an initial en-counter with raku—and indeed glaze ef-fects of all kinds—result from the com-bined endeavors of glazing *and* firing. It is in fact the phenomenon of postfiring re-duction that makes American raku unique. (This will be discussed in depth in Chap-ter 6.)

My glaze palette contains both a clear glaze and a white glaze. While a clear glaze will give you a good white when working with a truly white clay, the de-gree of whiteness is greatly enhanced by using a glaze containing tin or one of the other common opacifiers (opax, Superpax, Zircopax). You also have a choice between using a transparent glaze and an opaque one that has different effects when other glazes are used with it. I use the clear glaze when I wish to tone down the whiteness or when I want to affect other glazes and slips. A 5–10 percent addition of tin oxide to a transparent glaze will give you a very nice white. When substituting one of the other opacifiers, the general rule of thumb is to double it. Any more than that and you run the risk of ending up with a thick, milky effect. Commercial stains such as Mason Stains [or underglaze colors] are another good source of color in glazes. I suggest beginning with a 5 per-cent addition and then reduce or raise the amount according to taste.

Below is a compilation of glaze recipes

that comprises my current palette. Included are some comments regarding the *possible* effect of the particular glaze and a suggested thickness or application. Will you achieve the same results? Yes, no, maybe. If you already have considerable pottery experience, you know that using the same glaze recipe is only one step in an often futile attempt—and ultimately a meaningless effort—to duplicate another person's results. Even if you duplicate all the material and physical ingredients, there will still be innumerable reasons why my glaze does not come out like yours. Glaze application, the type of clay body, firing rate, personal idiosyncrasies in mixing styles, and atmospheric conditions in the kiln are just a few. Whether or not a certain glaze performs the same for me as it does for you is not the issue. The ultimate effect is what we are after. Use these glazes as suggestions, as jumping-off points. Your goal must be to develop a palette and vocabulary of your own. Only then will you be truly satisfied that your work is evolving and mandating the technique, and not that the technique is controlling the work.

I am always amused by potters who refuse to share a recipe, technique, idea, or observation for fear that their *originality* will be copied or stolen and the appeal of their work will be diminished. The selfishness of the "pottery freeloader" who is always willing to take but is not willing to give, or the potter who by working diligently through experimentation, failure, and eventual success in formulating a glaze feels that he or she has worked too hard to give it to someone else, will eventually hinder the growth of their work. Often the glaze came from a book, a friend, or a workshop, but they feel that it has become "theirs." I prefer instead to

share. I routinely give our recipes with the hope that other potters will reciprocate so that we can all expand our creative horizons. A recipe is nothing more than a tool, and just like a knife or brush, *it* does not determine the result—it is what *you* are able to do with it. Having enough faith and confidence in your own work and having gone through your own creative evolution allows you the freedom to share. So be generous with your knowledge, for we can all benefit.

Since my purpose is to give you a well-rounded and complete study of raku technique and not to list countless recipes easily obtainable from other sources, I have included a limited number of glazes, clay bodies, and slips. The glazes given here all mature within an acceptable range, and all have been tested. Among the books in the Bibliography are several very good sources of glaze, slip, and clay body recipes. One of the best books for understanding color development in glazes of all firing ranges, including low fire and raku, is *The Ceramic Spectrum* by Robin Hopper. In addition, *Ceramics Monthly*, the working potter's magazine, publishes more glaze recipes than could ever be used in a lifetime! I have tried to acknowledge the origin of the recipes, but recipes tend to become public domain after a while and their origins are difficult, if not impossible, to track down. My apologies to anyone I might have missed.

Del Favero Luster

Gerstley borate	80
Cornwall stone	20
Copper carbonate	2

A turquoise glaze that turns to a rich copper-penny luster under strong postfiring reduction. From Robert Piepenburg.

Yellow Crackle

Gerstley borate	80
Cornwall stone	20
Vanadium stain	3–6

A yellow glaze whose color depends on the type and amount of vanadium used. You can also add 5 percent tin oxide for increased brightness.

New Rogers Black

Custer feldspar	20
[potash feldspar]	
Gerstley borate	80
Red iron oxide	10
Cobalt carbonate	10
Black copper oxide	10

A dark blue glaze that develops a nice copper luster in strong postfiring reduction.

Gold Raku

Gerstley Borate	80
Cornwall stone	20
Tin oxide	1
Silver nitrate	2

A silver-gold glaze that is very reliable. Mix up only the amount you need and use it immediately. Silver nitrate is a soluble salt that is sensitive to light and will lose strength when mixed in water and exposed to light. See below for more information on the use of soluble salts. From Robert Piepenburg.

Basic White Crackle

Gerstley Borate	65
Tennessee Ball Clay	5
[HVAR ball clay]	
Nepheline syenite	15
Tin oxide	10
Flint	5

This is my regular white glaze. Apply it thick and you will get a nice bright, opaque white. Also a good base glaze to experiment with.

Rogers White

Spodumene	35
Gerstley borate	60
Tennessee ball clay	5
[HVAR ball clay]	

This is really a clear glaze. When used on white clay, it will be white! Apply thick. For a gray-blue glaze, add:

Red iron oxide	1
Cobalt carbonate	$\frac{1}{2}$

For a purple glaze, add:

Manganese carbonate	3
Tin oxide	5

Piepenburg 50/50 Red Bronze Luster

Frit 3134	50
Gerstley borate	50
Tin oxide	3
Black copper oxide	$2\frac{1}{2}$

A beautiful copper luster glaze. Under reducing atmosphere conditions, the result is a blood red. In strong postfiring reduction the result is a bronze-like copper luster. From Robert Piepenburg.

Higby 1-2-3 Base

Silica	1
EPK	2
Gerstley borate	3

Wayne Higby mixes this by volume, not weight. Another good clear base to experiment with.

Higby Water Blue

Frit 3110	70
Gerstley borate	5

Silica	5
Soda ash	10
EPK [kaolin]	5
Copper carbonate	3–6%

A beautiful blue-turquoise-aqua glaze that tends toward red when applied thinly and fired in reduction. The glaze will give copper flashes in postfiring reduction. For a lime green color, increase the copper to 8%.

Kemenyffy Opaque White

Gerstley borate	30
Frit 3110	30
Custer feldspar [potash feldspar]	25
EPK [kaolin]	5
Barium carbonate	5
Tin oxide	1
Hommel frit 373	4

Kemenyffy Gold Luster

Add the following to the opaque recipe:

Silver nitrate	1.5
Yellow ochre	1

Soda bicarbonate	2
Calgon water softener	$\frac{1}{2}$

Both Kemenyffy glazes are fired to cone $5\frac{1}{2}$, significantly higher than the other recipes provided here. The Calgon acts as a deflocculant, keeping the ingredients suspended and smooth without having to add too much water to the glaze. (See color Plate 4.)

Another type of glaze and technique is the so-called copper matt effect. Copper matt is a highly saturated copper mixture with just enough flux to melt it onto the surface of the clay. The effect is characterized by a highly iridescent, often inconsistent rough-textured surface and is achieved through a combination of correct thickness of the application, optimum firing temper-

3–9
Wayne Higby. Tower Land Winter. 1988. Landscape container (five boxes with lids), 15" h × 35$\frac{1}{4}$" w × 8$\frac{1}{2}$" d. Hand-built earthenware, raku fired and reduced in straw. Collection of Roger Robinson. Photo: Steve Myers.

ature, and appropriate postfiring reduction.

Mark's Copper Matt

Frit 3110	10
Copper carbonate	90
Iron oxide	5

Variation: Adding 2–5 percent cobalt and/or manganese can enhance color development.

My former assistant, Mark Dellorusso, is an expert in consistently reproducing the copper matt effect. More on his technique later.

Let's get back to experimentation and creativity for a moment. It is easy to understand why using glazes of the same maturing temperature is important, but how might you use glazes of different temperatures simultaneously? Remember, the only rules are the ones you want to follow. For instance, often as part of my glaze repertoire, I will use a variety of stoneware glazes in order to achieve certain color and texture effects. Stoneware glazes, you say? This idea came about accidentally. I was firing some student work and noticed the glaze on a piece in the kiln that was not melting with the others. Now, while this particular student was known for her nonconformity, this was obviously not what she had in mind. We took it from the kiln and reduced it in the normal fashion. Quite to our delight, the piece was wonderfully pastel, subtle, and very different from any previous raku results I had ever seen. There were some problems linked to this underfired surface—namely, the glaze was apt to flake. I was curious, though, and began to experiment with high-fire glazes in raku.

I am not talking about high-fire raku, only about using high-fire glazes in raku. Here are some tips. Use the high-fire glazes as you might use slips. Apply the glazes in a *thin* layer; thicker applications tend to flake more readily. Experiment with a thin wash of clear raku glaze (try any raku glaze) to act as a "sealer" over the high-fire glaze. Or apply the stoneware glaze over a thin wash of raku glaze. I have achieved interesting results with glazes in the cone 8 range containing copper, rutile, cobalt, and iron. Don't hesitate to use a high-fire glaze by itself, but I have noticed that heavy postfiring reduction makes the high-fire glazes dark and muddy; even so, don't take my word for it: try it. (See color Plate 6.)

How about the use of commercial glazes? These glazes can produce interesting effects, so go ahead and experiment. My objections to using commercial glazes exclusively are twofold. First, relying on any commercial material puts you at the mercy of the manufacturer. Second, and more important, you give up the most basic connection with your work—an intimate knowledge of your material. "Intimate knowledge" means different things to different people. For me, the lack of information is uncomfortable. I *like to know* exactly what I'm using. For instance, knowing the recipe of your clay body enables you to more easily adapt a glaze for a better fit. (The manufacturer will usually provide a list of ingredients when requested; if your supplier won't, then it is time to find a new supplier.) I use a commercially prepared clay body because I don't care to include clay-mixing facilities in my studio. Since I would be using a premixed clay anyway, it is logical for me to use locally available raku bodies instead of mixing my own custom recipe. As it turns out, one of the commercial bodies I tried possessed all the characteristics I was looking for: extreme plasticity, a very white color, a somewhat smooth texture, and a stoneware-range vitrification point. I suppose that when and if the manufacturer decides to drop the body, raise the price, or alter the recipe, I will have to make a decision, but I'll cross that bridge when I come to it.

Getting back to commercial glazes, wonderful effects are possible, and if you are going to experiment, then you might as well go wild. Try enamels, underglazes, overglazes, commercial slips—anything that looks interesting. Remember to pay attention to maturing ranges when firing commercial glazes with your own. (See color Plate 7.)

Glazes are clearly not the only means of achieving color and surface decoration on your pots. I have already mentioned the use of slips in the context of high-fire glazes and commercial slips. Slips can be used by themselves for texture and in some ways for color development as well. Generally, though, when thinking of slips in regard to color, it is not slips alone but rather the combination of the slips and the glazes you will apply over them that will allow you to achieve your desired result. Remember that in heavy postfiring reduction most unglazed surfaces will blacken. (I will go into detail in Chapter 6.) Although slips can be formulated for application on pots that are in the wet, greenware, leatherhard, or bisque state, I prefer to use slips at the time I make the piece—in the wet state. For one thing, it is far easier to formulate a foolproof slip to use for wet clay application. Also, from a design point of view, I prefer to decorate using slips while I throw.

The easiest and most surefire means of slip formulation for application in the wet state, and the method I use, is to use your clay body as the base for your slip. Dry out some clay, pulverize it, and add colorants to it by dry-weight percentages. If you begin with a white firing clay, any

colors are possible. If your clay is buff, tan, or darker, your slip may be limited in tonal range, but it's worth a try. Using your clay body as a slip base greatly simplifies your efforts.

Here are some slip recipes formulated for various states of application:

RISD Engobe

Cornwall stone	40
EPK [kaolin]	40
Frit 3124	15
Borax	5
Superpax [commercial opacifier]	10

This slip is for bone-dry ware. You can substitute tin oxide for Superpax by cutting the amount required in half. I use Superpax because it is much less expensive.

Higby Haystack Slip #5

EPK [kaolin]	25
Ball clay	25
Silica	20
Frit 3304	30

This slip is for leatherhard to dry ware and is a good base to add colorants to.

Kemenyffy White Slip

EPK [kaolin]	25
Kentucky ball clay	25
Custer feldspar [potash feldspar]	25
Frit 3110	20
Barium carbonate	5

Apply on leatherhard ware.

Slips can be used to achieve a very white surface on your ware. The whiteness will help you achieve the same kinds of results obtainable by using a porcelain clay body without the risk of actually using porcelain as your clay. It also will allow you to continue to use a particular clay body that works well in raku but may have an undesirable buff or tan color. The white, clean surface enables brighter colors and often a wider color palette. Try any porcelain slip and apply it when your piece is wet.

Oxides and stains may be used alone as washes both in combination with and without glazes. Oxide wash recipes are most easily arrived at through experimentation and recorded by volume measurement. Use the following measurements as a guide, keeping in mind that the final result will depend on your application technique, the clay body, and the other decorative materials you might be using.

Per pint of water:

$\frac{1}{2}$ tsp. copper carbonate: light green, turquoise
$\frac{1}{4}$ tsp. copper oxide: darker greens, blacks
$\frac{1}{8}$–$\frac{1}{4}$ tsp. chrome oxide: leaf green, opaque
$\frac{1}{8}$–$\frac{1}{4}$ tsp. cobalt carbonate: light blue, transparent
$\frac{1}{8}$ tsp. (or less) cobalt oxide: dark blue, black
$\frac{1}{2}$–1 tsp. red iron oxide: tan, brick red, brown
$\frac{1}{4}$–$\frac{1}{2}$ tsp. black iron oxide: opaque tan, brick red, brown
$\frac{1}{8}$–$\frac{1}{2}$ tsp. manganese dioxide: brown toward purple

3–10
Author. Vase. 1988. Wheel-thrown with combed texture. 18" h. Various oxide washes were applied by brush and then sponged together. A clear glaze covers the entire textured area. Photo: Robert Arruda.

Try whatever oxides you have using the above quantities as a guide.

Allow me to make an important suggestion that will help you arrive at desirable results and preserve your sanity at the same time. Keep a record of all experiments and write down all experimental recipes, as well as variations, permutations, and attempts at success. Write them down when you do them! Do this even if you change only one ingredient, alter only one percentage, or add only one new ma-

terial. Or how about this situation? You mix up a slip or glaze in a rush. You know exactly what you are doing—it's nothing new or different. You use it. You forget to label it. [*Move to the near future.*] You pull down a bucket of some familiar-looking stuff. "Is this that white slip I mixed up last time?" "Is this that glaze I added some tin oxide to last time?" End of story.

Further enhancement of luster effects can be achieved by using salts and so-called soluble salts. Some examples are bismuth subnitrate, copper sulfate, stannous chloride, barium sulfate, iron sulfate, and silver nitrate. These crystals or powders are dissolved in water and used as a wash or a spray over a glazed surface Silver nitrate can also be mixed into a glaze. Salts can be introduced into the firing chamber directly during firing or sprayed on after firing. (See Chs. 6 and 8.)

When using bismuth, stannous chloride, or silver nitrate as a spray or a wash, begin your experiments with 5 grams per cup of hot water. Mix the solution with a wooden stick or spoon or an old brush as these materials are highly corrosive, particularly bismuth subnitrate and silver nitrate. Another note: If you mix bismuth with any common salt (rock or table salt, for example), the chemical reaction will harden the resulting solution. Stannous chloride is moisture- and oxygen-sensitive. Open the container only briefly and keep it tightly sealed to avoid its breaking down and losing strength.

A common misconception is that a soluble salt becomes chemically altered and loses its strength in solution. What *solubility* actually refers to is the ability of the salt to be dissolved in water *without* an adverse reaction or chemical change taking place. Silver nitrate is light-sensitive and breaks down and loses strength when exposed to light. This is one reason for the confusion. Combine this with its high cost and you have two good reasons for preparing only what you will use at the time.

When using silver nitrate in a glaze, prepare a large batch of glaze in a dry mix without the silver nitrate. Weigh out just as much glaze as you need, mix with water, screen, and then add the silver nitrate. Apply the glaze or wash just before firing to take full advantage of its potency. If you have some mixture left over, store it in an opaque container out of the light. If the mixture turns a dark color, a chemical

change has occurred. Silver nitrate will stain your skin if not washed off immediately. Wear rubber gloves as a precaution. Stains on your skin are difficult, if not impossible, to remove. Try an abrasive soap like *Lava*. The stains will eventually wear away with no ill effects. Silver nitrate stains on clothing can usually be removed with *Spray 'N Wash*, found in the laundry section of your grocery store.

Copper, barium, and iron sulfate can be mixed in solutions of $\frac{1}{2}$ to 2 or more cups per gallon of water. In addition to applying them to the surface of your ware by spraying and brushing, try soaking your ware with these solutions and leave them unglazed.

Look through some scientific materials catalogues, or go to your local high school or college chemistry lab for these and other useful materials. If you introduce yourself and explain what you are looking for, you just may interest someone enough to help you out! Never use an unknown material before finding out about any possible hazards or adverse reactions that could be caused by your exposure to it. (See Materials and Supplies for more information.)

Glaze Application and Decoration

Often when the novice is unleashed into the excitement of the raku technique, that novice will be tempted to overglaze: too much glaze, too many different glazes, and enough copper luster to blind you. Instead, go for simplicity, spontaneity, and, ultimately, sophistication while you limit yourself to two or three glazes. The variety of effects obtainable through even a limited palette of glazes, as well as the black unglazed areas of the piece and the overlapping glazes, should keep you busy for a few years. Intelligent experimentation and comparison of results in raku, as in any glazing and firing method, requires consistency of technique. However, so many variables are integral to the raku process that complete consistency is difficult to say the least. Always take a patient, deliberate approach to the study of raku glaze effects.

Glaze application in raku generally follows the same rules as in any other pottery-making techniques. Glazes can be poured, sprayed, brushed, sponged, and dipped. For optimum effects, raku glaze should be applied on the thick side. Therefore, most of my glazing technique is centered around dipping and pouring. Because of the rapid fire, thick glaze application, and the ease of slightly overfiring, glazes tend to drip and run more than usual in raku firing. Be careful with your glazing toward the bottom of your pots. The danger is not that your pots will stick to the kiln shelf (remember, the pots are removed while the glaze is still molten), but the running and dripping glaze will make a mess of the shelf. You *can* achieve both a thick glaze application and be relatively sure of no glaze drips, so don't think that you have reached the catch-22 of glazing. One technique is to thin out your glaze application as you get toward the bottom of the pot. Another technique is to use liberal unglazed areas near the bottom. Some raku potters simply load their pots on old kiln-shelf scraps and the heck with the glaze drips. As you gain experience in firing and learn how to recognize a mature glaze melt, you will be able to glaze all the way down to the foot. Let your own aesthetic guide you.

The copper matt mixtures, on the other hand, do not melt like glazes and thus can be applied with less concern for dripping and sticking. In any case, they

3–11
One way to avoid glaze drips is to sponge off your glaze toward the bottom in a way that compliments your overall design.

are usually more effective when applied thinly—often so thin that you're sure that nothing will result. From an aesthetic point of view, copper matt can be used effectively in isolated sections on the surfaces or by itself on a piece without glazed areas overlapping onto the copper matt. Just one potter's opinion.

Applying glaze with a brush can yield interesting effects, providing you use high-quality brushes that allow you to apply heavy thicknesses of glaze. Often I hear students say they are sure they brushed on a glaze, but then there is litte evidence after the firing! More often than not, the application was too thin.

Try spraying glaze or oxides on your piece with a spray bottle or atomizer. The thickness achieved by using a spray bottle is not very substantial. Spraying is more effective when you want to apply multiple layers of glaze. Airbrushing with the appropriate equipment (airbrush and compressor) is the approach to take if you are serious about this process.

Resist techniques, such as wax, oil, and tape, as well as using stencils, are all common decorative approaches. Depending on the type of resist, you can brush, dip, pour, or spray your glazes. You can also vary the area that will be affected by the resist. For instance, tape can be re-

3–12

Douglas Kenney. Crackle Plate. 1989. Dry slips, clay, and porcelain, as well as copper filings, are pressed into the clay slab during forming. Glaze and underglazes are airbrushed. Intentional underfiring promotes additional textures and added crackle. 22" d. Photo: Eric Rippert.

moved after glazing in order to add another glaze over the taped area. Handheld stencils made of acetate or cardboard can be moved while spraying to vary the effect.

You may have come across the term "multiple firing" in respect to color and surface development. Multiple firing is a process of glazing and firing the same piece several times. High fire may be followed by a low-temperature firing, followed by a luster or enamel firing at an even lower temperature before achieving the final effect. Sometimes simply firing the same piece more than once at the same cone may alter the final effect of the glaze. Multiple firing techniques such as these may certainly be applied to the raku process. For example, a porcelain work previously glazed and fired to cone 9 may be raku fired (with or without the addition of raku glaze) for interesting color, crackle, and smoke effects. I mention this now because multiple firing can also be used as a technique for controlling your glaze or other coloring mixture application. Michael Sheba multifires two or three times in an electric kiln before the final raku firing to achieve his desired glaze effects. For Michael, the multifiring serves as an aid in masking so he can clearly see the previous layer of glaze. Then he can apply the appropriate stencils, such as cardboard, acetate, or tape, precisely. In this way the previous layer is not marred and the subsequent layer can be applied accurately. (Fig. 3–13 and color Plate 11.)

In addition to achieving color through combinations of materials and application techniques, the surface of your clay can have an effect on the final outcome as well. Heavily textured surfaces can be glazed and then washed, leaving the glaze in the crevices of the texture or carved de-

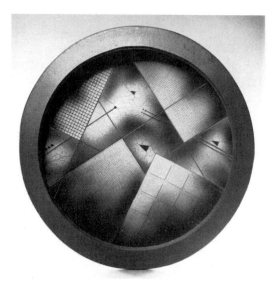

3–13
Michael Sheba. Raku Plate. *Hand-built with wheel-thrown rim. Impressed textures and airbrushed slips, glazes, and terra sigillata. 21″ d. (See color Plate 11 for detail.) Courtesy the artist.*

3–14
Geoffrey Pagen. Ceramic Wall Relief. *1988. Brushed glaze with dry glaze application. The dry glaze imparts a uniquely textured surface both tactically and visually. 12″ h × 10″ × 10″. Courtesy the artist.*

signs. By using a wide brush over a textured surface, you can avoid getting the glaze in the textured areas and apply it only to the raised part of the design.

Textures can be incorporated into the glaze itself to reveal nuances of color and appearance. Geoffrey Pagen applies a dry mixture on the surface of his wall reliefs composed of 1 scoop of glaze and 2–3 scoops of 30-mesh silica sand. Since the mixture is dry and does not adhere to the surface, loading the work into the kiln must be done carefully so as to not disturb the placement of the mixture on the piece. Upon maturity, the glaze, with the silica imbedded in it, has fused onto the ware, producing an appearance that bridges that of a glazed surface with an unglazed one. (Fig. 3–14 and color Plate 8.) The result

varies depending on the glaze used and the extent of the postfiring technique.

Remember that raku is primarily a firing process, and while successful work is always the result of the combined efforts of forming, decoration (if applicable) and firing, you should not restrict your approach to glazing and surface embellishment. In short, no glazing method should be excluded from your raku repertoire, and you should explore any means of personalizing your glazing and decorating style.

Because of the strong image the "raku workshop" occupies in many potters' minds, the glazing process is invariably thought to *immediately precede* the loading and firing of the ware. While this is frequently done, it is often at the expense of

3–15
David Powell. Wheel-
Thrown Vase. *1990. 22" h.*
After firing, Powell sand-
blasts selected areas of his
pieces using 50-mesh silica
sand as the sandblasting me-
dium. In some cases the
glaze is completely blasted
off the piece, leaving dry,
matte effects with the heavy
crackle from the remaining
glaze. Courtesy the artist.

the successful glazing of the ware. Glaze that is still wet on a piece as it is placed to preheat, or loaded into a hot kiln, will crack and flake off. Allow the glaze to dry on the piece, preferably overnight, before commencing with the firing.

Fine lines exist between technical expertise, unbridled expression, and aesthetic success. Even if you are experienced with other firing techniques, you will find the raku process unpredictable, seemingly uncontrollable, and possibly frustrating. But I hope you will also find it refreshing. Be patient and allow yourself to grow into raku. You will achieve success on all fronts.

Kilns

Chapter 4

As you are beginning to see, though there are certainly rules that govern right and wrong and keep you on the right track, raku is a technique that is flexible and to a certain degree accommodating—accommodating, that is, to many of the various parameters that would ordinarily confine us in conventional firing. Suitable glazes and clays, for instance, can span a rather wide range, and kiln designs that are appropriate for raku include an equally wide variety. Just about any fuel, including electricity, can be used to power your kiln. Also, the size and shape of the kiln can vary tremendously, as can the refractory material used in kiln construction.

Kiln building can be an intimidating part of setting up a pottery studio. Even a potter with only a basic knowledge of kilns knows that crucial to the success of a kiln design are the relationships between interior dimensions, flue size, stack height, primary and secondary air intakes, and Btus—quite a formidable list. For electric kilns that list includes watts, volts, amperes, wire size, and coils. Fortunately, the design requirements of a raku kiln, whether electric of fuel burning, are infinitely simpler and more forgiving than their larger counterparts.

Before thinking about kiln design, you must decide on the type of fuel you want to use. Kilns are classified according to fuel used in addition to the style of construction. But the most basic limiting factor is the fuel you want to use, and here you have two choices.

Electric Kilns and Raku

If you know that you cannot accommodate a fuel-burning kiln, whether because of space limitations, zoning restrictions, or for some other reason, you may think that you will be excluded from the world of raku. Let me be the first to dispel this notion by telling you that you *can* fire raku in an electric kiln. While it's not the all-around best, the most flexible, or the most versatile, an electric kiln is clean, relatively safe, and sometimes is considered to be the easiest and most convenient kiln to use depending on your studio. The reason potters often separate electric kilns from other types of kilns is that all the factors that go into designing, powering, controlling, and ultimately knowing your kiln are similar whether you use natural gas, bottled gas, wood, oil, or any other fuel. Electric kilns, on the other hand, are quite different.

Building a fuel-burning kiln is within every potter's ability and budget, while building an electric kiln is not. How can I say that when each of us knows someone who has built an electric kiln? And if building an electric kiln is impractical, why have books and articles been written to tell you how? One reason that some potters consider building an electric kiln impractical is that important aspects of construction must be dealt with, such as calculating the correct resistance for the coils, knowing what wiring is appropriate, and then, of course, fashioning the coils as well as shaping bricks to accept the coils. Among other things, these factors require special skills that are often beyond those of the average potter. When you take into account the effort, time, and cost and the overall quality of the result, it obviously makes more sense to purchase an electric kiln for raku rather than build one.

If you already have some raku experience, you may say, "That's all well and good, I can fire in an electric kiln. But then how will I possibly be able to produce the wonderful spectacle that raku is known for?" Briefly, raku doesn't have to be a community-rousing event!

All electric kilns are basically the same. The current of electricity causes resistance wire to heat up, and when the heat is transferred to the atmosphere in the chamber, sufficient temperatures are reached. The resistance wire—the *elements* or *coils*—are controlled by switches that either vary the *amount* of current to the elements or vary *how often* the current passes through the elements.

Electric kilns can be top-loading or front-loading and can range in size from about half a cubic foot in volume (for enameling or jewelry work) to 12 cubic feet. (Figs. 4–1, 4–2, 4–3.)

Using an electric kiln for raku is essentially no different than using a fuel-burn-

4–1
Typical multisided electric kiln.

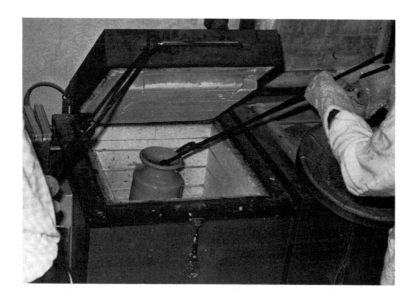

4–2
Square top-loading electric kiln.

ing kiln, although you must make some adjustments. Foremost, you must protect yourself from contact with the electric current in the elements themselves. I have seen elaborate setups that involved muffles or saggars in the kiln chamber that physically separated the potter from the coils. Not only does this make unnecessary work, but it decreases the interior dimensions of the kiln. The most practical way to isolate yourself from the current is to shut off the kiln before you reach into it.

An electric kiln is well insulated, vents a minimum of hot exhaust gases, and heats up and cools down slowly. While

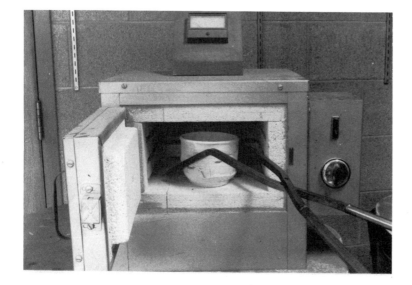

4–3
Small enameling kiln.

these are some of the inherent advantages of using an electric kiln, unfortunately they prevent the raku potter from firing multiple loads; which is one of the attractions of raku firing. Firing multiple loads depends on whether you can preheat the next load of ware (usually on top of the kiln using escaping heat and exhaust) and have immediate temperature control to be able either to raise the temperature slowly or quickly. This is not possible with an electric kiln.

Finally, the cumulative effect of exposing the elements and bricks to rapid heating and cooling, as well as the harsh use of the kiln hardware, such as the lids' handle and hinges, and the increased exposure of the hot face of the lid to room temperature all serve to decrease the life of the kiln. How much? Well, certainly not enough to discourage you from doing raku if all you have is an electric kiln. In fact, you can take measures to minimize the harsh effects on the kiln:

- Use a gentle touch when opening the lid or door of the kiln.
- Lower the lid down, or close the door carefully so you don't inadvertently subject the bricks of the lid, door, or walls to any rougher treatment than necessary.
- Stack your pots no closer than 2" to the side of the kiln. This will help eliminate the possibility of touching the brick with molten glaze when you lift out your pot.
- Stack your ware as close to the top of the kiln as possible using a kiln shelf. This makes it easier to reach in to remove the ware with less likelihood of touching an interior surface with either tong or pot.
- When removing your pots, open the kiln only as much as necessary to min-

imize temperature shock to the hot bricks.
- On a top-loader, use tongs to grab the handle and open the lid. Do this carefully and securely without bending or otherwise mangling the handle.

These procedures will be described in detail when I talk about firing (Chapter 6). I have been raku firing in an electric kiln for years with minimial damage to the kiln. In fact, there are some clear advantages to using an electric kiln for raku. Since most cracking occurs during the heating cycle because of raising the temperature too fast, the slow, even temperature rise of an electric kiln automatically takes care of that for you. It's slow for sure but essentially foolproof! Tending of the firing is minimized: turn it on high and after one firing you will know exactly how long it will take, usually two to three hours in a typical electric kiln. If you soak your glazes at the end of the firing to achieve particular effects, an electric kiln is ideal. Simply turn the switches down to medium and soak to your heart's content. An electric kiln is clean and requires little in the way of special preparation. You don't even need special electrical service if you purchase a small kiln that operates on standard household current (100–120 volts [UK: 240 volts]). If you maintain your kiln yourself, that is, change the coils and switches, replace crumbled bricks and worn-out hardware and don't plan on doing raku every day of the year, an electric kiln will have a long, productive life and not be much worse for the wear from raku.

Whether or not you plan on raku firing in an electric kiln, you should learn basic kiln repair and maintenance. Potters should strive for as much self-reliance as possible. The goal is not to become iso-

4–4
Patrick Crabb. Conical Reliquary II. *14" h × 27" l × 10" d. Using a combination of electric firing and gas firing, this piece was first fired in an electric kiln for glaze and color development. When cooled, it was reheated to low red heat in a gas kiln and reduced in newspaper, carefully avoiding contact between the paper and the glazed areas. Courtesy the artist.*

lated and completely self-sustaining but rather to achieve a degree of independence from otherwise uncontrollable situations that ultimately will affect our work. You don't want to have to reschedule a firing and disturb a work plan while waiting for a kiln repair service to replace a burnt-out coil or a bent lid hinge.

Fuel-Burning Kilns

Do you need to build your own kiln? The answers is no. With the number of commercial kilns on the market, you cannot help but find one that will meet your needs. Commercial raku kilns have usually been of ceramic fiber design built over some sort of a wire frame and set on top of a soft brick base (Fig. 4–5). Often included in the package is the necessary combustion equipment (burner, hose, regulator) and sometimes even the empty propane tank. The ceramic fiber design is a good one, but let me say two things. First, you can build this kiln yourself at a

4–5
Expanded-metal fiber kiln package manufactured and sold by Miami Cork and Supply. Courtesy the manufacturer.

considerably lower cost. Second, and understand that I am not a do-it-all-yourself kind of guy (remember, I use commercial clay!), you can gain a great deal of knowledge by building your own kiln from scratch. Choosing the correct combustion equipment is invaluable in understanding how your kiln works, how to control its firing, and ultimately understanding the entire raku process.

Other types of commercial kilns either specifically designed for or suitable for raku include sectional soft brick, updraft kilns designed for all firing ranges; larger, fiber-built gas kilns in the 10-cubic-foot range or smaller; and popular sectional electric kilns that can be adapted for gas firing when their useful lives as electric kilns have ended. I will discuss each of these types of kilns as you learn how to

4–6
Model 18 insulating brick raku kiln manufactured and sold by Summit Gas kilns. Courtesy the manufacturer.

What every potter's been waiting for . . . a kiln that bisques, high fires (Cone 10), reduces, and best of all is especially designed for raku work. It's clean, efficient, and effortless.

The Olympic 3.29 cubic foot raku kiln operates on either natural gas or propane. It measures 17½" wide by 22½" high. The top 18" of the firing chamber can be easily elevated by the turn of a hand winch. This allows easy access to the firing chamber while trapping the heat in the kiln and away from the operator, thus eliminating the need for expensive protective clothing while Rakuing.

The Olympic Raku Kiln comes with a one-year warranty. Shelving and an ignition ring-thermocouple safety shut-off are available options.

OLYMPIC KILNS
6301 Button Gwinnett Drive
Atlanta, Georgia 30340
Phone (404) 441-5550

4–7
Raku kiln on overhead lift-off track with hand winch. Courtesy Olympic Kilns.

design and construct them yourself. Each one has its strengths and weaknesses depending on your particular situation. Commercial kilns in general are perfectly fine, but they are costly and you are bound by certain sizes and configurations. Unless you embark on building your own, you will be at a disadvantage when you need to make a repair or alteration.

Basic Combustion Theory

Fuel-burning kilns can be fired with bottled gas (propane or butane), wood, oil, coal, and charcoal. Propane is a plentiful fuel that is simple to use. Wood is the preferred fuel of the purist. It is the most traditional fuel and is appealing because it has a purity and romanticism attached to it. Some potters insist on using wood for raku in order to keep modern technology at arm's length. Similar sentiments exist about coal and charcoal. Selecting a fuel can almost be considered philosophical, and its a question you must answer for yourself.

With the advent of bottled gas and simple, efficient burner systems, gas has replaced oil as the potter's fuel of choice. For the raku potter who is looking for convenience, nothing beats gas. It is clean, efficient, and easy to master and control. In addition, the raku potter often needs to be able to dismantle the kiln or at least the burner system after each firing. This is easy to do with a gas system and not so easy (or even possible) with an oil system.

Although I will focus primarily on propane and wood, combustion theory is applicable, with some adjustments, to other fuels. Other factors that pertain to combustion theory include burner type and size and the dimensions of the flue opening and burner port (or firebox). Combustion theory is important to discuss at this stage because later, when we get into kiln building, the reasons for certain dimensions and other design considerations become more evident and sensible when one has some knowledge of combustion.

In fuel-burning kilns, combustion is the activity that ignites and directs your fuel. Probably the most crucial information to learn is the relationship between air and fuel. This is also the most misunderstood phenomenon to most novice potters. I have seen situations where a kiln is well designed and well built, the burner is more than adequate, and the fuel supply and pressure are fine, but no matter how long the kiln fires, the glazes just won't melt! Invariably for the inexperienced rakuer, the first thought that comes to mind

4–8
Len Eichler. Conglomerate Vessel #21. *1989.*
Raku fired and reduced in straw; the press-molded and thrown components are reassembled, pressed, and attached within a larger master mold to give definition to the outer shape. 24" h × 13" × 12".

is that the glazes have been mixed incorrectly or they mature at higher temperatures. I have prevented many batches of perfectly good glaze from being trashed because I know that in most cases the problem is simply not enough air getting into the kiln. Fuel needs air to burn. Not enough air and the flame will only get so hot. Too much air and a cooling effect takes place, resulting in not enough heat production.

There are four opportunities for air and fuel to mix: primary air, secondary

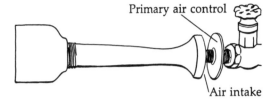

4–9
Typical venturi burner showing primary-air control and intake.

air, flue, and what I call incidental air. Strictly speaking, all the air that mixes with the fuel after ignition is secondary air, regardless of where it enters the kiln, but these four terms are convenient for a better understanding of the firing process. The first three are sources that we want to be able to control, but first a brief word about the fourth—incidental air. This is air

that enters the firing chamber through cracks in the walls, spaces between the bricks, or through a loose fitting lid. The initial effort in building a kiln is to eliminate these openings as much as possible. Once the firing is under way, if you need to minimize any openings that should occur you can stuff them with small pieces of refractory fiber. (But watch your fingers.)

Primary air enters the burner and mixes directly with the fuel before combustion. Figure 4–9 shows the primary air intake of a typical venturi burner. Secondary air enters the kiln through the burner port in the space around the burner or open peep holes.

Let me differentiate right now between the often incorrectly substituted terms *flue*, *damper*, and *stack* and note how they func-

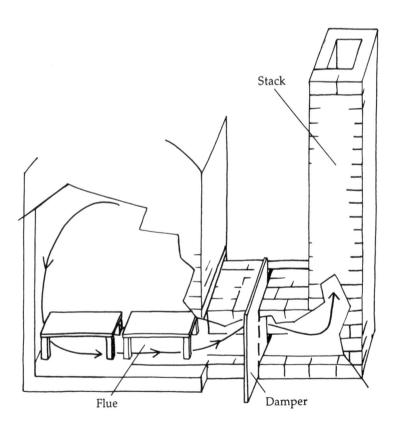

4–10
Typical flue, damper, and stack of a fuel-burning kiln showing the pathway of air and gases.

tion. The flue is the passageway between the firing chamber and the stack, as shown in Figure 4–10. (*Stack* and *chimney* are interchangeable terms.) The damper allows you to control the amount of gases and heat entering the stack and ultimately the amount of draft in your kiln. *Draft* is the flow of gas and flame in the kiln and, because it ultimately controls the air-fuel mixture it must be adjustable. The greater the draft, the greater the sucking action of the kiln through all of its openings, especially the secondary air sources. The more air that is allowed to enter, the greater the air-fuel mixture. In the simplest raku kiln, where there is no chimney, I use the term *flue* to refer to the opening at the top of the kiln, which serves the same purpose as a stack. (I will explain how to best control and adjust these air sources when I talk about firing in Chapter 6.)

Now let's add another variable to the

4–11

Simple flue and damper in an updraft raku kiln. The flue is the opening in the top of the kiln; the broken kiln shelf serves as an adjustable damper that slides over the opening.

combustion theory: atmosphere. Changing the amount of air mixing with the fuel affects two things: temperature and atmosphere. Atmosphere refers to the kind of flame—whether oxidizing or reducing. An *oxidizing* flame is characterized by a blue color, which indicates that it is clean and burning efficiently; it is the result of plenty of air mixing with the fuel. An electric kiln of course offers the same clean atmosphere. Any fuel-burning kiln will produce *some* carbon, which results from imperfect combustion, so a strict, ideal oxidizing atmosphere is not possible. For all practical purposes, though, an effective oxidizing atmopshere doesn't have to be the ideal one.

A *reduction* flame is characterized by a yellow color and inefficient burning—the result of too little air mixing with the fuel. A reduction atmosphere is possible to achieve in an electric kiln by introducing organic materials such as wood or coal. Unless you have a well-ventilated kiln area, however (in which case you can probably accommodate a gas kiln), you should avoid doing this. Otherwise you would need to have a drawer or opening at the bottom of the kiln. (Premature coil failure is also a result of reduction in an electric kiln.)

In raku, as in other types of firing, you want to be able to achieve both oxidation and reduction atmospheres at the appropriate time. An oxidizing flame and atmosphere is necessary for temperature advance; a reduction atmosphere is necessary if you want glaze effects that can be achieved only through reduction firing. The point is to have the most efficient operating system you can while still giving you the greatest flexibility and control.

Gas-Fired Kilns

With a gas-fired kiln, as long as the burner is large enough and you make provision for primary and secondary air sources, everything else can be adjusted easily; you can even adjust many times during the actual firing. The burner port should be about 2″ larger in diameter than the burner. Thus, if the burner is 3″ in diameter, make the burner port at least a 5″ square. The flue should be about 1½ times the area of the burner port. For example, if the burner port is 25″ square, the flue opening should be about 40″ square, or 6½″ × 6½″. Larger openings are always preferable to smaller ones. Unless you are building a true downdraft kiln, you do not have to worry about a stack or chimney.

Two factors are crucial when choosing the correct burner system for your kiln: the construction material used for the kiln, which will determine the approximate heat input in Btu's per hour per cubic foot needed, and the interior volume. To arrive at the volume or cubic feet, use the following calculations:

Cylindrical kiln:
$\pi(3.14) \times radius^2 \times height = volume$

Rectangular kiln:
length × width × height = volume

All dimensions must be in the same measurement. If your dimensions are in inches, divide by 1,728 to convert to feet.

The recommended refractory materials and the corresponding approximate heat input needed in Btu/hr/cu. ft. are:

1″ 8-lb.-density refractory fiber blanket: 30,000
2″ 8-lb.-density refractory fiber blanket: 15,000
2½″ G-20 A.P. Green insulating firebrick: 32,000
4½″ G-20 A.P. Green insulating firebrick: 18,000

(These are examples only and not an endorsement of A.P. Green products.)

Under no circumstances should you use hard fireback for your kiln, except for the floor and around the burner port. Hard brick has little or no insulating value and requires an enormous heat input to reach temperature. To apply the above information, note the following examples: For a cylindrical 1″ × 8-lb.-density fiber-lined kiln, 20″ diameter × 33″ high (inside dimensions):

$3.14 \times (10)^2 \times 33 \div 1,728$
$= 6$ cu. ft. $\times 30,000 = 180,000$ Btu/hr

The 30,000 figure corresponds to the requirements for using 1″ × 8-lb.-density fiber blanket. You would then need a burner system that would deliver the necessary 180,000 Btu/hr.

For a rectangular 2½″-thick insulating firebrick kiln 18″ × 18″ × 27″ high (inside dimensions):

$18″ \times 18″ \times 27″ = 8748″ \div 1728$
$= 5.06 (5.1)$ cu. ft.

5.1 cu. ft. $\times 32,000 = 163,200$ Btu/hr

You can see that this is not as difficult or complicated as it may seem. What we can surmise from these equations is that the more energy-efficient your construction materials, the smaller your burner system will have to be, the less gas you will use, and the faster you will be able to reach temperature for both the first firing of the day and for multiple loads thereafter. Keeping fuel expenses down should be a good incentive for building an efficient kiln. In other words, the more firings you can do between having your propane tanks refilled, the better!

Several raku burner systems for propane designed and sold by Harry Dedell in Vermont are illustrated in Figure 4–12. Harry is widely acknowledged as an expert at designing kilns and burner systems. He recommends a Ransome B-3 sys-

Plate 1

Raku Sonyu (1664–1716). Black raku tea bowl named Eboshi. *$3\frac{6}{16}''h \times 4\frac{5}{8}''d$. A magnificent example of the raku ideal made by the fifth-generation Kichizaemon. A soft, leathery surface of black to brown coloration upon a gentle undulating rim and body. Courtesy the Art Complex Museum.*

Plate 2

Chojiro (1516–92), the first generation of the Raku Family. Red raku tea bowl named Nokitsuni (Wild Fox). *$3\frac{5}{16}''h \times 3\frac{11}{16}''d$. The faded, red matt glaze is characteristic of many of Chojiro's red bowls. Courtesy the Art Complex Museum.*

Plate 3

Attributed to Raku Donyu (1599–1656), the third-generation Kichizaemon. Black raku Tsutsu *tea bowl. $3\frac{3}{4}''h \times 4''d$. The shape is identified as* tsutsu *(cylinder). The piece was intended as a winter bowl; the tall, narrow circumference retains the heat of the tea. Donyu is famous for developing the bright luster and thick flowing glazes that characterize later raku and for which it became so well known. Courtesy the Art Complex Museum.*

Plate 4

Susan and Steven Kemenyffy. Autumn Louise.
*48"h × 30"w × 8"d. Raku sculpture decorated with
a variety of glazes, both commercial and homemade.
Courtesy Susan and Steven Kemenyffy.*

Plate 5

Author. Bowl. *13"h × 13"d. 1988. Poured glaze,
reduced in sawdust and reoxidized. Photo: Robert
Arruda.*

Plate 6
*Author. Vase. 20"h. 1988. Combed
surface, poured stoneware glazes with
wide brush strokes of cobalt raku glaze.
Photo: Robert Arruda.*

Plate 7

Michael Hough. Juxtaposed Frenzy. *40″ × 30″.
1990. Tile mural. The individual tiles are cut from a
single slab roughly formed in the shape of the final
piece. Commercial glazes are used exclusively, with
the exception of the occasional use of a homemade
copper luster. The finished tiles are glued to a plywood sheet with a commercial adhesive. Courtesy the
artist.*

Plate 8

Geoffrey Pagen. Wall Relief. 31"h × 21"w × 2"d.
1986. Commercial and homemade glazes, reduced in
coarse straw. A silicon carbide masonry blade was
used to cut into the bisque ware before glazing.
Courtesy the artist.

Plate 9

Wayne Higby. Emerald Lake. 14½"h × 34½"w ×
8½"d. Five boxes with lids. Textures from contact
with the straw reducing material are evident, as well
as heavy crackle on the edges and corners resulting
from stress on the glaze. Photo: Steve Myers.

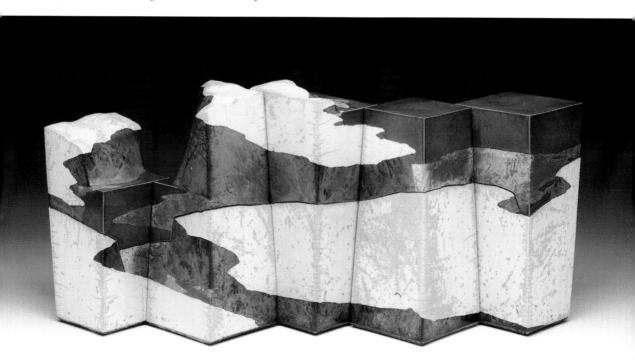

Plate 10
Mark DelloRusso, Vase.
$6\frac{1}{2}''h \times 5\frac{1}{2}''w$. 1988. Copper
matt glaze (see recipe) re-
duced in dry leaves.

Plate 11
Michael Sheba. Raku Plate.
Detail of Figure 3–13.
Courtesy the artist.

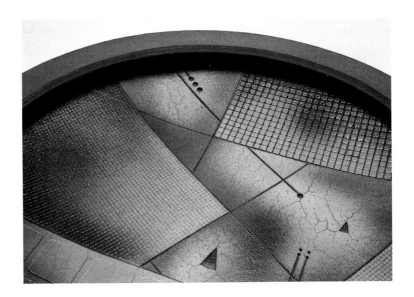

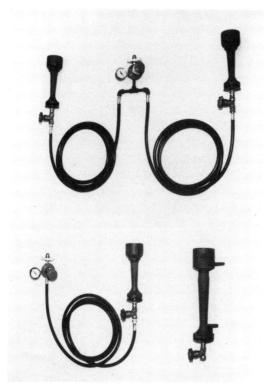

4–12

Raku burner systems complete with burner, valve, hose, high-pressure regulator, and gauge designed and sold by Harry Dedell. (Top) dual burner system operating off of a single tank. (Bottom) Single burner to operate off a single tank. Other configurations are also possible. Courtesy Dedell Gas Burner and Equipment Co.

tem for kilns requiring up to 125,000 Btu/hr and a B-4 system for up to 250,000 Btu/hr. Depending on the shape and design of your kiln, a dual burner system may be more appropriate and efficient than a single burner. Because most raku kilns are in the 10-cubic-foot range or smaller, I have found that a single burner system is sufficient. The gas pressure of propane should be set at approximately 7–10 p.s.i. and can be adjusted for maximum efficiency.

Propane is a bottled liquefied gas available in tanks of different sizes. The 20-pound tank used with outdoor gas grills is the most common. This size tank is perfectly adequate for small kilns, say up to 3 or 4 cubic feet, when no more than three loads are fired successively and the weather is warm. What does warm weather have to do with raku firing? A propane tank low on gas tends to freeze. When this happens, the gas pressure drops and your firing will all but stop. To avoid this predicament, use the largest tank possible for your circumstances. As an additional measure, you can manifold or gang two (or more) tanks together effectively and double or triple your fuel capacity. Your local gas supplier should be able to outfit you with the proper hoses and fittings to accomplish this. Even taking all these precautions, freeze-ups can happen, especially if you are firing in cold weather. The remedy is to pour hot water over the tank and fittings until the firing is finished. (*But do not turn the tank over on its side. If you do, you run the risk of withdrawing liquid instead of vapor—a dangerous situation.*)

If you get involved in working on a large scale and need a larger kiln to fire four, five, six, or even more loads at a time, or you need to fire two kilns simultaneously, manifolding small tanks together still may not give you a sufficient fuel supply. At this point you will need a larger tank. The other readily available sizes are 30-, 40-, and 100-*pound* tanks and 250 and 500-*gallon* tanks. Why are some sized in pounds and others in gallons? Tanks up to and including 100 pounds are considered portable and are labeled in pounds (for lifting and carrying). A 40-pound tank weighs about 70 pounds when full. A 100-pound tank is approximately 150 pounds full. Larger tanks (250 and 500 gallon) are stationary and labeled by their

4–13
(Left) A 30-pound propane tank. (Right) A 40-pound propane tank set in a plastic milk crate for stability.

capacity in gallons. For volume comparison, 4.84 pounds equal one gallon of gas.

I recommend using a 40-pound tank; it holds a reasonably high volume of gas and is truly portable. Usually I gang two 40-pound tanks together. I keep a few 20-pound tanks as spares.

While 20-pound tanks are readily available at hardware stores, lumberyards, discount stores, and even some supermarkets, the 30-pound or 40-pound sizes will probably have to be ordered from a bottled gas company. For raku, 100-pound tanks are great because their capacity seems bottomless. Unfortunately, they are not easy to transport and it could be dangerous to do so. Aside from the sheer weight of the tank when full, they are large and require a truck for transportation. The only practical way to use one is to lease it from the gas company, which will refill it on short notice. I once paid a yearly lease of about $20 for the tank, and having that extra capacity was terrific.

Suppliers of gas, tanks, and accessories differ greatly in what they offer and in their knowledge about bottled gas. For tanks and gas, shop for the best value.

4–14
A 500-gallon propane tank.

Some suppliers charge a set price per tank/per fill up, regardless of whether the tank is empty. Others charge you only for the amount of gas you buy. Most lumberyards and hardware stores are familiar only with 20-pound tanks and may not know what to do with a 30- or 40-pound tank. Make sure your supplier knows what he is doing before you allow him to fill your tanks. To avoid a potentially dangerous situation, make sure you know the capacity of your tanks.

Propane tanks are filled by weight less about 20 percent for expansion. A 20-pound tank weighs about 18.5 pounds empty. Add that to the weight of the gas and you have the total full weight. A tank's empty weight, or tare weight, is stamped on the ring around the top of the tank. (Fig. 4–15) A 30-pound tank weighs about 25 pounds and a 40-pound tank about 30 pounds. Exact weights vary ac-

4–15

The protective collar on top of a 40-pound propane tank. The tare weight (T.W.) is 31 pounds and is stamped into the collar.

cording to the manufacturer. Propane tank valves are equipped with an automatic pressure-release mechanism in the event the tank is overfilled or when warm weather causes the gas to expand. If the mechanism is activated while your tank is in storage, outside of course (you will hear a hiss or see gas being emitted), open the valve for a few seconds to relieve the pressure.

Your best source for hoses, fittings, pressure regulators, and other specialized components is someone who speaks your language, like Harry Dedell in Vermont or a pottery supplier that carries combustion equipment. Local gas companies can provide a rich source of equipment as well as information. Here in Newton, Northeast Cryogenics supplies bottled gas of all types to hospitals and manufactuers. The company is experienced in all phases of gas supply and has been helpful and given me all kinds of information on equipment. The point is that you can seek out suppliers that do not necessarily cater to potters. You will know quickly whether they are knowledgeable, understand your needs, and are interested in helping you. Many times the simple fact that you are a potter intrigues them and they will be willing to help. Commercial plumbing supply houses can also be good sources of equipment, but in my experience they tend to have little patience with nontrades people. If you see a sign that says "Homeowner's: Go to the back of the line," they probably will not be interested in helping you find the correct hose for ganging your tanks. The more you know about what you need, the wider your range of sources becomes.

The advantage of natural gas is that it offers a "bottomless tank." If you sometimes operate on a moment's notice, that can be a real lifesaver. Tank storage is no longer a problem, and using natural gas indoors is safe providing you are equipped with the proper safety devices. However, to take advantage of natural gas, your site must be near a public gas line. Realize too that the cost of setting yourself up will be higher because you will need permanent and rigid plumbing connections, which must be done by a licensed plumber. This also reduces the flexibility you have in moving or in rebuilding or altering your kiln, which is often as much a part of the raku process as making and firing the pots themselves.

To use natural gas, the kiln must be built close enough to the gas line to avoid pressure drop, assuming that your meter size and piping are sufficiently large. When using natural gas, power burners—that is, burners with electric blowers attached (Fig. 4–16)—are preferable to venturi-type burners and are more expensive. Have a service representative come out and give you some figures. Weigh the advantages and disadvantages, compare the

4–16
Natural gas burner with blower, thermocouple, and safety shutoff attached. Courtesy Johnson Gas Appliance Co.

costs of plumbing and equipment, and then make your decision. I'll tell you, though, it's hard to beat not having to worry about a frozen system or running out of fuel.

Wood-Fired Kilns

Wood is an elemental fuel that needs few requirements in the way of equipment— no burners, tanks, or hoses. Just an ample firebox, ash pit, ax, and a supply of wood—and of course plenty of stamina and brawn and an unwavering dedication to the firing process! If you have the opportunity, give wood a try, but realize that whatever wood firing lacks in equipment and cost is more than made up in the effort required to prepare the wood and fire the kiln.

For proper combustion, wood requires a large firebox, one that exposes the wood to maximum oxygen to ignite it and allow it to give off its energy quickly. Wood, like any solid fuel, burns from the surface. Therefore, smaller pieces of wood fire hotter and give off more heat than do larger pieces. Firing begins with large pieces of wood; smaller pieces are used as the firing progresses.

The wood should be thoroughly dried (about a year) to prevent the release of steam from the wood into the chamber. Steam can have a cooling effect on the firing, which could prevent the kiln from reaching temperature. Softwood is preferable to hardwood as a fuel because softwood is less dense and thus burns faster. Using wood as a fuel is so integral to the firing process itself that I will reserve any further discussion for the chapter on firing (Chapter 6).

Coal-Fired Kilns

Several different types of coal can be used in a kiln. *Anthracite,* the coal used for home heating, is hard, slow burning, has little to no sulfur content or emissions, and is clean burning. Anthracite is available in approximately ten different graded sizes and looks like random-size rocks. *Bituminous* coal, of which there are several varieties, is used in industry and is what has been traditionally used to fire kilns. It is softer and also is available in graded sizes, as well as dust and powder.

True charcoal is a wood product and not related to coal at all. To produce charcoal, wood is heated in a kiln in the absence of oxygen; the charred result is hardwood charcoal, an all-wood product shaped in either natural lumps or briquettes. Briquettes are formed by combining the smaller pieces and dust left over from the manufacture of the lump charcoal, using wheat starch or glucose as a binder. Briquettes burn longer than lumps, but lump charcoal definitely burns hotter. Charcoal briquettes found in supermarkets and hardware stores are *not wood,* but are made from a coal base and contain petroleum bonding agents and fillers. These briquettes do not burn as hot as either of the natural wood products. For our purposes, any form will work, but natural lump hardwood charcoal is preferable. For the ecology minded, true hardwood charcoal is a much cleaner burning fuel than common charcoal briquettes. For a source of hardwood charcoal, look in the Yellow Pages under "Charcoal" or try a wholesale restaurant supplier. A 40-pound bag costs about $15.

Kiln Construction

The size and complexity of kilns can vary over a wide range. They might have elaborate welded steel frames and hinged doors or be built on rails as in car kilns or built with overhead lift-off devices. Most kilns, however, do not need such complex design elements and are simple enough to be within the reach of most mortal potters. In fact, construction techniques are relaxed and design specifications flexible.

Once you have decided to build your own kiln, you will want to follow certain strategies. The first of these strategies should be to match the design of the kiln to the kind of work you want to do. Consider such basic questions as the size of your pieces, whether you want to be able

4–17
Fiber-lined trash-can kiln and homemade burner built by Dick Lehman. Note the long handles for easy lifting; the kiln shelf serves as the damper. Courtesy Dick Lehman.

to fire multiple loads or do one firing at a time from a cold kiln, and whether you prefer a top-loader, front-loader, or even a car kiln. The last thing I want to do is confuse the issue and make doing raku more complicated than it has to be. Many of these considerations are more pertinent to the advanced raku potter who is ready to do some customizing and fine-tuning.

The second strategy applies whether you build your own kiln or purchase it. Where you are going to locate the kiln? As they say in real estate, the three most important factors in determining the value of a property are location, location, and location. It is just as true for your raku kiln. Ideally you want to choose a location that is safe for the firing and raku processes and one where your freedom of movement will be completely unencumbered. An outdoor location for your kiln and postfiring facilities lends itself naturally and easily to the raku process. If, however, you find yourself in a situation where either the firing or the smoking phase, or both, cannot be carried out outdoors, you are not necessarily out of luck. For instance, you already have an electric kiln that cannot be moved outside, or you don't have an outside area in which to work at all.

While not all circumstances are adaptable to raku, with a little ingenuity, *most* are. Figures 4–18 and 4–19 show the kiln area at Thayer Academy. The room is concrete block with a cement floor and the kilns are close to a wide double door that opens to the outside. Ware is removed from the kiln and carried outdoors, where the postfiring takes place. A more complex situation where both the firing and smoking had to be carried out indoors was solved by the Radcliff Pottery Studio. (Fig. 4–20) Not only is the kiln vented to the outdoors, as it must be, but the postfiring

reduction is carried out in an enclosed chamber that is also vented to the outside. This ingenious and unique facility was designed by Nancy Selvage, director of the studio. The reduction chamber is constructed of galvanized sheet metal and features a Plexiglas sliding door fashioned from a stock sliding window unit found at a home supply store. While both examples are far from ideal, they do allow raku facilities where otherwise they could not exist. You can see that the problems in locating your raku facility indoors are many, and if given the choice, building indoors is often not worth the trouble. Enough space to work comfortably, ventilation, fire detection and prevention, and general safety are but a few of the issues.

Let's limit our discussion to *raku alfresco*. In placing the kiln, consider safety first. Place the kiln away from any structures, low hanging tree limbs, or any other physical obstacles that could get in your way and impede motion and activity around the kiln. After siting the kiln for safety, consider how you will operate the kiln. Is the kiln as close as possible to the studio door so that you can carry pots and equipment to it easily? Do you want to be able to see the kiln from your studio window? Will you need electricity at the kiln site for lights or to feed a power burner? Do you have a convenient source of water nearby? Is the kiln site safe and secure from curious passersby and onlookers?

Regarding construction, will the kiln be a permanent structure? Most raku kilns are not considered permanent. In fact, kilns in general are for the most part movable. Figure 4–21 shows a true "mobile kiln." In practical terms, though, the larger and more complicated the kiln—with external frames, tall stacks, and arches—the more permanent it is. For planning purposes, even though they are

4–18
Kiln room at Thayer Academy. Note the close proximity of the kilns to the wide double doors.

4–19
Outside the kiln room at Thayer Academy, where postfiring is carried out.

4–20
Raku kiln and post-firing reduction chamber at the Radcliff Pottery Studio, Allston, Massachusetts. Note the venting ducts from both the kiln and reduction chamber.

4–21

Because he couldn't set up his kiln in a permanent outdoor location, Michael Hough designed a soft-brick kiln with a fiber-lined refrigerator lid and built it on a metal base with wheels. This allows him to wheel it out to fire and wheel it back into the studio for storage. Courtesy Michael Hough.

easily moved, I think of my kilns as permanent, thereby eliminating one variable from the equation. These are just a few of the types of "functional" concerns you should keep in mind when deciding where to place your kiln. Now let's get to a few technical concerns.

Building a Top-Loading Soft Brick Kiln

Tops on the hit parade of easy-to-build kilns if the top-loading soft brick rectangle. It is simple in design, expandable, adaptable to various styles of firing, and very serviceable. I prefer top-loading kilns to front-loaders for several reasons. The

4–22

Soft-brick kiln with corbeled arch at the Wesleyan Potters, Middletown, Connecticut. Note the use of an electric kiln lid with its hinge pivoting vertically on a steel rod attached to the angle-iron frame of the kiln.

height of a top-loader can be varied easily by simply laying on another course of bricks. There is nothing more frustrating than discovering that your pot is 1″ taller than the kiln. All of the pieces loaded into a top-loader are visible at once when you remove the lid. Being able to see all of the pots greatly facilitates the unloading process. In a front-loader, if you want to remove a particular pot and it happens to be in the rear of the kiln, well, you see what I mean. For design and construction, no special skills are needed; the door of a top-loader doubles as the lid without the need for hinges and metal frames. In a front-loader you need to construct a vertically hinged door. I have seen front-loaders where the door was actually taken down and put back up brick by brick after each firing!

Another consideration is the heat given off by the kiln when it is opened. Both types of kilns give off a terrific blast of heat when the door is opened. However, when unloading a top-loader, you can shield yourself from the heat by looking into the kiln from a slight angle while reaching in with your tongs. The side of the kiln itself acts as a heat barrier. When unloading a front-loader, there is no getting away from the heat. You have to stand directly in front of the kiln with this heat blast coming right at you. One advantage a front-loader has over a top-loader is that you can use shelves for stacking pots, which means that you have the ability to fill the kiln much more efficiently.

Your first task is to decide how wide and deep to make the chamber. You can determine this by the size of the kiln shelf you will use and the dimensions of the soft brick. The brick we are working with is $4\frac{1}{2}″ \times 9″$, so for simplicity the kiln is de-signed in multiples of $4\frac{1}{2}″$. Our plans call for an $18″ \times 18″$ interior dimension, for which we can use a readily available $16″ \times 16″$ kiln shelf.

The next task, after kiln size, is to situate the kiln relative to the nature of the site—for example, the nature of the topography and terrain (sloping, hilly, rocky, soft earth). These are important considerations regardless of the type of kiln you build. Wind direction will have a direct bearing on managing and controlling your fuel source, so if possible, position the kiln in a way that allows the wind to blow *toward* and *into* the burner port. (More on this later.) Locate the kiln away from low hanging tree branches and any vegetation that might be affected by the heat.

Whether you are building one or buying one, decide now if you want it to be ''permanent'' rather than simply sitting on a metal base, as most electric kilns do. For permanence, you will need some sort of foundation. The ease of constructing a foundation depends on the composition of the ground. The most durable and permanent base is a concrete slab. Doing this yourself is a rather ambitious undertaking, and to have one poured professionally is expensive. Here's some advice, though, for constructing a slab base: Make it large enough to accommodate at least twice as many kilns as you think you are likely to need. Once you go to the trouble and expense of contracting or doing this work yourself, you'll find it is much less expensive to do it all at once rather than piecemeal. The slab serves as a smooth, level surface upon which you can erect your kiln, accommodate your bottled gas supply, and even do all your postfiring work. In place of a concrete slab, the ground itself serves quite well.

The actual base of the kiln, whether

you use a concrete slab or the bare ground, is comprised of concrete blocks. These blocks are manufactured in many different sizes and shapes, so it's possible to configure a base to exacting specifications. I use the standard 16″ × 8″ × 8″ builders block. (The true measurements are $\frac{3}{8}$″ less for each dimension to make up for the thickness of the mortar joint when doing real masonry.) This size block is heavy enough to provide a firm base and raise the kiln to a comfortable height. Because it's compatible with brick measurements, you can construct a neat installation.

When purchasing concrete blocks, notice the difference between end or corner blocks versus stretcher blocks. The corner blocks have flat tops and good square edges as opposed to line blocks, which are designed to butt together and have the empty middle area filled with concrete for strength. Since we will not bond the blocks together with concrete, we will use corner blocks, which give a much neater and finished look to the base.

While I'm on the subject of neatness it pays to go to the trouble of making your kiln area look and even feel nice. Doing this will probably affect your work in positive ways. Sometime ago a potter rented a small workspace at The Potters Shop. The 10′ × 10′ space contained a wheel, table, shelves, and other assorted potter's paraphernalia. One day, about a week later, I noticed outside the studio a pair of rubber fishing boots caked with clay, the kind that go up to the thighs. When I looked inside, I could see that this potter wore these boots while he was working. I also noticed clay everywhere—on the floor, walls, and shelves. Even his wheel was camouflaged by clay. When he gave up the shop and left for parts unknown, I undertook the task of cleaning and recover-

ing the space and furnishings as though I were on an archeological dig. Layer after layer revealed some new evidence that some living, working creature once inhabited the area. So be forewarned: neatness counts!

After laying out the design for the base of the kiln on paper, set the concrete blocks on the ground and level them as you go. A bucket of sand will help in the leveling. If you are building on grass, first remove the sod. Set the blocks tight up against each other and level from all directions to ensure a smooth surface. A garden spade is a good tool for this kind of work. The square, flat end facilitates smoothing the ground for the blocks. Place each block firmly on the ground; the block should not rock. Stand on it and tamp it down to set it firmly. Place the blocks so that the holes are toward the outside. This will provide a solid, smooth surface on top and also serve as a vent for the hot air under the kiln.

Make your base larger than the footprint of the kiln so that you will have a place for preheating pots, cooling pots, and for other objects that you will need to be close by. Next comes a layer of soft insulating brick. On top of that is the layer of hardbrick that will serve as the bottom of your kiln. I use hardbrick because it is durable enough to withstand the abuse of placing work on it, standing on it, and knocking onto it, as potters are wont to do.

What kind of soft brick should you use? If cost is a problem and you have some K-20 brick or its equivalent (2000°) around the studio, then by all means use it. This brick is serviceable for the temperatures of raku. If, however, you will purchase bricks expressly for this project, then the logical choice are bricks between 2300° and 2600°. The K-23s offer better in-

4–23
Setting the base of our soft-brick kiln using sand and dirt to level the blocks. Note the level used to be sure all is true. The concrete blocks are corner blocks.

4–24
Stamping on the blocks to settle the base.

4–25
Soft-brick subfloor in place with a hard-brick floor being laid.

4–26
Cutting soft brick using a whole brick as a guide.

4–27
The first two courses of brick and the burner port in place. Three posts are set for the kiln shelf, with one post in front of the burner port to split and direct the flame.

4–28
The kiln shelf in place, level with the top of the burner port.

4–29
Laying subsequent courses of brick. Note the concrete block and bricks in place at the burner port ready to receive the burner.

4–30
Completed firing chamber with peepholes in place.

4–31
Safely cutting the angle iron with a saber saw.

4–32
Stainless-steel hose clamps ganged together and tightened down around the kiln.

sulating properties, while the K-26s are more durable. Use the K-23s for their insulating properties.

Depending on the dimensions of your kiln, you will have to do some cutting, so before we get too far along in the building let me say something about tools and cutting bricks. Don't let the softness of the brick fool you. While soft bricks are easy to cut, they will dull even the best saws, knives, and drill bits. Use inexpensive tools when working. Be sure to protect your eyes from airborne particles when cutting bricks. Most cutting will involve simply cutting the bricks in half. Since bricks are twice as long as they are wide, use another brick as a cutting guide. (See Fig. 4–26) The next step is the actual laying of the firebrick for the walls of the kiln. The first course of bricks will have to incorporate a burner port. Note in the illustrations the construction of the burner port. For durability and strength, use a

hard brick for the lintel, the brick over the top of the opening.

Before continuing with the kiln, put your kiln shelf in place. There are different schools of thought regarding the best functioning kiln shelf. Some options are a clay or silicon carbide shelf set on kiln posts; the same shelf set on hard bricks, which also act as a mechanism for directing the flame; or hard bricks themselves. I use silicon carbide or clay shelves (depending on what I have around) set on posts, with one acting as a target brick. The target brick is placed in front of the flame to split the flame and direct it to both sides of the chamber for even heat distribution. (Fig. 4–27) Using hard bricks as your shelf greatly increases the amount of mass that needs to be heated, which lengthens the firing and increases fuel consumption. Whatever you use as a shelf, be sure that its top is just above the burner so that all of the flame goes underneath. (See Fig. 4–28) You want to isolate your pots from direct contact with the flame. A major cause of cracking of pots in the firing is direct contact of the ware with the flame.

Continue laying the bricks, course after course, staggering the joints for strength until the kiln is the height you want. Theoretically the kiln can be any height, but if the ratio between the width and height is too great the heat between the bottom and top of the kiln will be uneven. As a general rule, keep the height to within 1½ times the inside width. It's a good idea to leave one brick removable every couple of courses, alternating the side of the kiln. This brick serves as a peep hole for monitoring the firing from different angles and heights.

As a final step, you can tie the kiln together with a series of corner braces and cable or pipe clamps. Doing this will allow the kiln contract to its original size after firing. This step is optional, for in practice this size kiln will not expand too much and can be pushed back together easily if it does. Installing corner braces is not difficult. Pick up some steel angle iron at your local hardware store. It is inexpensive and can be easily cut with a saber saw or hacksaw. (Fig. 4–31) I love stainless-steel hose clamps (also available at the hardware store) because they are strong and last forever. The clamps can be ganged together to form a band as long as you like and can be tightened down firmly. (Fig. 4–32) If you use cable, then you must use a turnbuckle to tighten the cable. Cable and clamps are probably equal in strength, so use whichever you want.

A firm, stable support must be provided to hold the burner in place. This is a good opportunity to liberate the Rube Goldberg in you, clamping all kinds of braces and stands around the burner. A

4–33
Adjustable burner stands designed and sold by Harry Dedell. Courtesy Dedell Gas Burner and Equipment Co.

good support can be fashioned easily from a soft brick. Using the burner as a template, carve and file out a groove in the brick for the burner to rest in, as shown in Figure 4–34.

The next phase is the construction of the kiln lid. The lid can be made from any extra kiln shelves you may have lying around the studio, and in fact these are what I have always used. As a lid, kiln shelves have proven to be durable, strong, and reasonably insulating. Using two

4–34
Soft brick carved out for use as a firm burner support.

shelves allows the space between them to act as an adjustable flue opening.

Next on my hit parade of lids is a refractory fiber lid made from wire mesh and fiber. It is easy to construct, lightweight, easy to remove, and reasonably durable. I found an interesting product called "Gro Thru" in a commercial landscaping and garden supply store. This wire mesh circle is designed to be placed over new plantings to protect them as they grow. It comes in different diameters and is perfect for covering with refractory fiber to use as a kiln lid. Discarded metal refrigerator shelves and barbecue grills also can be covered with fiber. Or use an old electric kiln lid and simply cut a hole through it for the flue.

A lid can also be constructed of individual fire brick tied together with rods and angle iron. This lid is strong, lightweight, and has good insulating properties. If you plan to have help with your firings, build your lid in one section with handles for two persons to lift. If you anticipate firing on your own, build the lid in two halves to facilitate its removal by one person. You will need predrilled heavy-duty angle iron, $\frac{3}{8}''$ or $\frac{1}{2}''$ threaded rod, nuts, washers, and lock washers—all available in hardware stores. The rods and angle iron keep the bricks together by compression. Cutting the angle iron a little longer than necessary allows it to function as a fine handle. (See Fig. 4–35) You must drill holes through the bricks so you can pass the threaded rod through them. Fashion a cardboard template and use it as a guide in drilling the holes rather than having to measure each brick individually. Assemble everything on a flat surface and loosely attach all the hardware. Tighten the nuts evenly, going from one to the next so you don't end up with a tight row of bricks next to a loose row. Upon com-

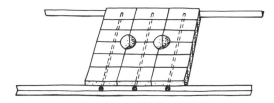

4–35
Soft-brick kiln lid. You can substitute straight steel or some other stock for the angle iron.

pletion, cut out the flue openings. Because the bricks will naturally expand and contract during use, make a habit of checking the tightness of the nuts periodically.

Building a Fiber Kiln

A fiber kiln is closely associated with raku. Refractory fiber has brought kiln building within the reach of many people who otherwise would have been too intimidated by the need for steel frames or complicated brick work. The kiln is simple in concept and construction, as well as being lightweight, truly portable, and reasonably

4–36
Refractory materials are available in many different forms. Pictured here is 1" fiber blanket, 2" board, and a procelain fastening stud. Photo: Jim Neely, Thermal Ceramics Corp.

durable. I say "reasonably" durable because it cannot be exposed to the elements
without reducing its lifespan. Thus you
should enclose it under a protective structure or tarp or bring it inside after each
use. You must be careful to not allow your
pots to come in contact with the fiber because the glaze melt will tear the fiber
from the kiln.

Because the fiber is not resistant to
abrasion, you may want to apply a rigidizer to the interior surface. Rigidizer is
available from ceramic fiber dealers. Apply
it according to the manufacturer's instructions, usually by brushing, rolling, or
spraying. Also, you cannot change the
height of a fiber kiln conveniently as the
brick kiln described above. The height of
the kiln can be no lower than the height of
the fiber chamber itself. However, if you
accept these few idiosyncrasies, a well-
built fiber kiln will serve you well and has
the potential to last a long time. My small
fiber kiln (Fig. 4–37) has been fired more
than 1,000 times and is still going strong.

Before beginning construction, you
must determine how tall and wide you
want to make the fire chamber. A metal
trash can or some sort of hardware cloth
or wire mesh are the usual materials for
the frame of the chamber. I prefer hardware cloth or wire mesh because it is versatile as a building material, lightweight,
and easy to fabricate. Another type of wire
mesh that is useful is called *expanded metal*,
used for fabricating safety guards on ma-
chinery and as space dividers in trucks,
among other things. This material, available at metal scrap yards and steel suppliers, is much stronger than mesh and
provides a rigid yet lightweight frame for
your kiln. Expanded metal is sold in 4' ×
8' sheets and is available in various thicknesses and diamond sizes. You can decide
which gauge is appropriate for your kiln.

4–37
*A fiber kiln constructed of heavy-gauge hardware
cloth and 1"-thick refractory fiber.*

Whatever you use, avoid any material that
will be too flexible and not hold its cylindrical shape well, such as chicken wire.

Your material list will include:

- 1" × 8-pound-density fiber for the
  lining
- $\frac{1}{2}$"-thick refractory board to fashion
  buttons and strips for attaching fiber
- Kanthal or nichrome wire for sewing
  the fiber to the frame
- Two aluminum sash handles with
  bolts, nuts, and washers for securing
  them to the frame.

Optional supplies include rigidizer and

4–38
David Powell's expanded-metal fiber kiln. A cable on pulleys attached to a brick counterweight makes lifting the kiln easy. A gasket of fiber acts as a seal along the bottom of the kiln.

porcelain buttons used as an alternative means of attaching the fiber to the frame.

The diameter of the kiln will depend on your needs, the kiln shelf size, and the design of the base. For a brick kiln, shelf size is usually the logical determining factor. Common shelf diameters are approximately (depending on the manufacturer) 17″, 23″, and 26″. A fiber kiln wide enough to accommodate a 26″ shelf would be too large to maneuver easily, so I suggest either of the other two sizes. Our kiln here is 20″ in diameter to fit a 17″ or 18″ shelf. This kiln functions comfortably atop a simple brick base, built as we did the first few courses of the brick kiln. The slight modifications necessary to make a square base suitable for a round shelf and kiln can be accomplished by inserting a shaped brick

in each inside corner of the base. (Fig. 4–39) Another alternative is to recycle an old burnt-out section from an electric kiln, cutting an opening for the burner. (Fig. 4–40) This has the advantage of being portable and is already bound together for strength. Whichever type of base you choose, be sure to match its dimensions with those of your chamber.

Begin building the fiber kiln by constructing the frame itself, including handles for lifting, and the roof. Thick material (expanded metal, for example) can be welded if you have the skill, the equipment, or a friend who can help you. A local welding shop can do this for you inexpensively, or better yet, see if you can coax the industrial arts or shop department of the local high school to help you

4–39
An expanded-metal fiber kiln at the Rhode Island School of Design, Providence. A brick is positioned in each inside corner of the base to accommodate the round chamber.

4–40
A burner port cut into a section from an electric kiln.

out. You can never be too resourceful! If welding is not an option, sew the metal together with wire or bolt it with small screws and nuts, as I have done in Figure 4–42). Remember, though, that the reason for using this material or wire mesh is that it's both easy to work with and light-weight, so don't get carried away and use some super-heavy-gauge metal that is too difficult to handle.

With the cylinder formed and open at both ends for easy access to the interior, attach the sash handles with bolts, wash-

ers, lock washers, and nuts, locating them about midway up the chamber. Cut a piece of the material for the roof of the kiln and attach it with wire. (Fig. 4–44) Small angle braces spaced 6″ or so apart is another effective method of attaching the top to the cylinder. (Fig. 4–49) As you fasten on the top, *be careful to keep the chamber as round as possible.* Cut out an opening for the flue, centering it in the top. Depending on the height of the chamber, decide on the number and location of peep holes. Three at different heights and spots around the chamber are usually adequate.

Once the wire frame is complete, you are ready to line it with the fiber blanket. *Safety Alert:* Regardless of how hot the weather is, wear a long-sleeve shirt, gloves, long pants, and mask when working with fiber blanket. The fibers are extreme irritants that at the least will make you itchy and uncomfortable. Use the chamber as a template and cut out a sec-

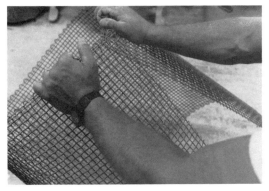

4–41
The chamber is formed out of a flat sheet of expanded metal or, in this case, heavy-gauge wire mesh.

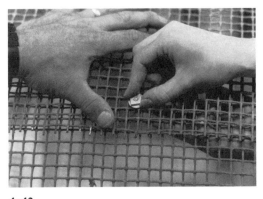

4–42
The chamber can be secured effectively by using small nuts and bolts.

4–43
Aluminum sash handles are lightly hammered into a slight curve to conform to the shape of the chamber and attached with screws and nuts.

4–44
One method of attaching the top is to tightly twist wire.

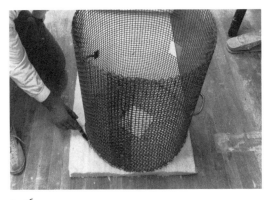

4–46
Trace the chamber on the blanket with a felt-tip marker. Cut the blanket with a mat knife or shears.

4–45
The completed metal chamber with flue and peepholes cut out.

4–47
Cut buttons from 1" rigid insulating board. Insert a kanthal wire "staple" through the button.

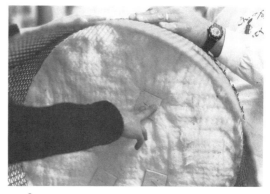

4–48
The staple with button is pushed through and held tightly against the blanket, then twisted around the outside of the wire frame.

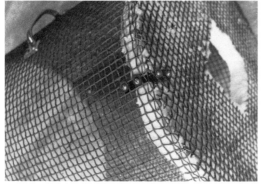

4–49
The fiber secured to the top of the chamber. Note the angle brace (colored black for clarity) as an alternative means of attaching the metal top to the sides of the chamber.

4–50
Cutting the ends of the fiber at a bevel will assure a tight fit around the chamber.

4–51
Lay the fiber in the chamber gently, being careful not to compress it or to release the irritating fibers into the air.

4–52
The completed fiber kiln on a recycled electric kiln base.

tion of fiber for the roof using a matt knife or shears. Although the fiber is a strong material, it tears easily, and because it lacks a real *fiber* quality, it cannot be sewn. The several different fastening systems that are available (Fig. 4–53) are too large and expensive for our application. I use a system (patterned after the commercial one) of buttons or strips cut from rigid insulating board to fasten the blanket to the frame. Lightweight, 17- or 18-gauge kanthal or nichrome wire is inserted through the button, fiber, and frame. (Fig. 4–48) The ends of the wire are then twisted together tightly. This system is simple, neat, and effective. Heavier wire is too thick to twist easily. Instead of buttons, you can cut strips about 2″ wide and install them vertically. The strips give an added measure of rigidity to the structure. As an alternative to the board, you can fashion stoneware or porcelain buttons as some potters have done. I have never used them, but I'm told they work just as well.

Measure the interior circumference and height of the chamber and cut out your blanket. Bevel the end cuts as in Figure 4–50. When you butt the ends to-

4–53
Various commercial anchoring and fastening systems for refractory fiber materials. Courtesy Thermal Ceramics. Photo: Jim Neely

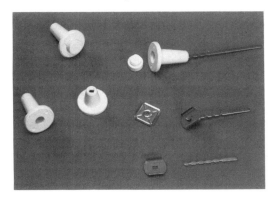

gether, the beveled edge will form a tight, smooth connection with no thick fiber overlap. Lay the blanket inside the cylinder and, using the same method as above, attach the blanket to the wire frame.

The number of buttons you use in attaching the fiber and the amount of space between them are not critical. Use enough buttons to prevent the blanket from draping or sagging. Needless to say, too many buttons are better than too few. Try them every 8–10″ apart. They are easy enough to remove and reposition if you have to. For the flue and peep holes, simply trim the fiber close to the opening and secure it with buttons and wire. There is no need to cover these exposed edges of the frame with fiber.

As a final step, as I mentioned earlier, some potters apply a rigidizer to the inside of the kiln. This liquid solution imparts a hard, rigid surface that will minimize abrasions and prolong the life of the blanket. I have spoken to several potters who have had good success with rigidizer, but I found the rigid surface was too thin and was susceptible to cracking due to the lifting of the chamber, the extreme hot and cold variations, and the general rough treatment that the kiln will be subjected to. I suggest skipping this step and using rigidizer only if after several firings you find that the surface of the blanket is giving you problems.

Finally, place your chamber on the base you have just built (see page 67) and you're ready for firing.

Recycling an Electric Kiln

My raku kiln of choice is one made from recycled electric kilns. (Fig. 4–54) They are generally well built, lightweight, stackable for increased height, and available in a variety of widths. If you live in an area with many potters or a supplier that does kiln repair, then chances are there are burnt-

4–54
Typical multisided electric kiln recycled as a gas-fired raku kiln. This kiln is 27″ w × 31½″ h (interior dimensions) and is powered by a Ransome B-4 burner with 7–10 p.s.i. of propane.

out, ready-for-the-junkyard orphans of kilns that are just waiting for you to take them away. I have literally gotten electric kiln shells for nothing; I have also paid up to $30 for a 24″ × 9″ decagon kiln section, so don't be surprised if you have to pay. But if you approach your regular supply house in a friendly way, you may be able to coax someone there into letting you take an old kiln off their hands. Don't be greedy and expect the electric parts to be intact. Somebody probably has salvaged those already. All you really want are the brick sections wrapped in their fine steel jackets. Also try to find a lid and bottom, but if you can't, they are easy enough to fashion yourself.

Once you have kiln in hand, you must make some accommodation for the burner.

One approach is to place the kiln on top of three or four courses of brick with a burner port incorporated into it, as in Figure 4–28, but what I like about recycling an electric kiln is that it makes a neat and complete unit by itself. For this you need to cut a burner port into the side of the kiln. Draw a square on the steel 3″ wider than the diameter of your burner. Locate the square about 2″ from the bottom of the chamber. This is important because if you cut too close to the bottom of the kiln, the thin sliver of brick that remains under the burner port will soon crumble, leaving no brick there at all. Using a $\frac{5}{16}$″ bit, drill a hole inside the square near one of the corners as a starting hole for a pair of tin snips. Insert the tip of the snips into the hole and carefully cut on your outline.

(Figs. 4–55 and 4–56) With the steel cut away, trace the burner on the brick, enlarging it by an inch or so. Using a drywall saw, insert it through the brick anywhere within the square, saw up to the outline, and cut out the brick. You can finish it off neatly using a course wood file. I have left a space between the actual burner port as it goes through the brick and the steel jacket (Fig 4–40) to separate the flame from contact with the steel as much as possible, thereby increasing the life of the steel jacket.

With the burner port in place, now simply set the chamber on the floor (which could be the bottom of the original electric kiln if you were able to obtain it) and put a shelf on posts so that it sits right above the height of the burner port, thereby keeping the flame under shelf and away from direct contact with the ware. Here, as in all of my kilns, I place a post

4–56
The brick exposed with the burner traced onto it. Photo: author.

with its edge direcly in the path of the flame. This splits the flame in half, directing each half to the opposite side of the kiln to ensure more even heat distribution in the chamber.

If you are using the lid that came with the kiln, you must cut a flue hole. Draw a circle in the center of the lid $1\frac{1}{2}$ times the diameter of the burner port. Using the same drywall saw technique, cut out the hole. No, the bricks will not collapse, but periodically check the tightness of the band that holds the lid together. Finish off the lid by attaching two aluminum sash handles or a second sash handle opposite the one that might already be on the lid.

Here are some other useful tips when using a kiln of this type. Typically, the peep holes that are standard with electric kilns are too small to be useful for much of anything. Enlarge them with the tin snips. A soft brick cut to size serves as a plug. One of the features of this type of kiln that I like and often take advantage of is the relative ease with which you can remove a section or two when the firing is

4–55
Use straight, high-quality tin snips (Wiss brand in this case) to cut through the stainless-steel jacket of an electric kiln. Photo: author.

complete to make removing pots easier or to expose the lower portion of the interior. I will do this when I want to lift out a tall pot. I find it easier to approach the pot from the sides rather than from directly on top of it. To do this, simply attach at least two large sash handles to each section of kiln.

Building a Wood-Fired Kiln

My first raku kiln building and firing experience was with a wood-fired kiln. Crazy, you say? Absolutely. Doomed to failure?

4–57

Wood-fired, top-loading raku kiln built by Hal Riegger in 1973 using common red bricks, local clay, sawdust, and gravel. Courtesy Hal Riegger.

No question about it. Certain to discourage you from ever doing raku again? For sure. Now to complicate matters further, I had never built a kiln of *any* kind before. And the final test of my insanity? I had never actually observed, let alone participated in, any kind of raku firing from start to finish! I went to work on the kiln with only a vague idea of the process, a sketch of a kiln given to me by a fellow graduate student, Geoff Pagen, all the bricks and materials I needed supplied by the prep school where I was student teaching. Watching me was a herd of believing high school students and art teachers who thought I was a pottery god. Needless to say, that first wood-fired kiln was a resounding success. But I was lucky. A few weeks later, with the help and participation of some fellow graduate students, I built an identical kiln at a different site. No matter how much wood we stoked, we couldn't reach temperature. At the time I had no idea what was wrong. It was only after many more firings of all kinds did it become clear that it was a simple case of poor combustion due to a lack of appropriate air sources. If only I had had this book!

Wood is the most basic source of fire and heat. Wood is true to tradition. Wood is romantic. If there is a drawback to wood firing, we might as well begin with it. Aside from having an appropriate place to locate a wood kiln, that is, away from civilization, firing one is a lot of hard work. While there is no question that the effects of wood firing are hard to duplicate, whether in high fire or raku, you have to decide whether the effort that has to go into building and firing one is worth it. Aside from the gathering and cutting the wood and stoking constantly to keep a kiln going, the major drawback for me is the inability to be spontaneous when

4–58
Woodpile ready to fuel a firing. Four or five loads of ware can be fired with this quantity of wood. Photo: author.

doing raku. More often than not, I decide to do a raku firing almost on the spur of the moment or, if I really plan ahead, the night before! Having to resign myself to an all-day affair of chopping wood and stoking the kiln would definitely cool my fire. Having said that, though, let's go ahead and build a wood kiln.

The structure and dimensions of the firing chamber of a wood kiln are essentially the same as the kilns already illustrated. The differences are in the accommodations that must be made for using wood as fuel instead of gas. A conventional burner port is replaced with a firebox, and making provisions for a proper primary air source and efficient combustion is absolutely essential. This means constructing a large enough firebox and flue. Note that the firebox and firing chamber of the kiln in Figure 4–59 are

4–59
Fire box, ash pit, and lower portion of the firing chamber. The kiln shelf is in place and is level with the top of the firebox. Photo: author.

both dug into the ground. By doing this, we provide ample combustion space and a place for the ashes to collect. We can also utilize the insulating properties of the earth and take advantage of the fact that hot air rises if we keep the combustion area at a lower height than the firing chamber. A wood kiln can be built level on a conventional concrete-block base.

Building a wood kiln, or any kiln for that matter, is an exercise in resourcefulness, for in addition to firebricks you will need some iron bars or grating for the wood to rest on, as well as material such as old kiln shelves, lintel bricks, sheet metal, or spanning tile for roofing the firebox. Of course we could go to extremes and build a form for the construction of a formal arched firebox, but we are on an austerity budget and want to keep this project within the reach of every potter. Try your local metal scrap source or junkyard. Even if you have to pay, you should be able to escape with minor financial damage.

Using Figures 4–59 and 4–60 as a guide (no need to be concerned with exact measurements), dig the firebox/ash pit 27–30″ below the level of the ground at the opening. A hard brick lining is more for support and structure than for insulation. Soft insulating bricks are preferable for the firing chamber, though as a cost-saving measure many potters recommend using common red bricks for the entire structure. Theoretically, within the temperatures reached in raku firing, common red bricks should be quite serviceable. However, I have used them (as in the kiln pictured here) and find that even in the relatively low temperatures of the firebox, the bricks can spall and become a physical hazard as they crack apart and explode.

Set in 3 or 4 iron bars 4–8″ apart to support the wood during firing. Keeping the wood suspended on the grating allows for a clear flow of air around it to promote combustion. The end of the firebox should come up to the level of the floor of the firing chamber, which itself is set into the ground approximately 9″ or so. The floor of the kiln can be made of firebrick set directly on the ground or the brick can be set over a concrete block. The only advantage the block affords is a more solid structure that is somewhat easier to make level. Build up the height of the firebox to approximately 8″ above ground level. Us-

4–60
Completed wood kiln. The firebox has been topped with kiln shelves and covered with earth. The chamber has been built up to the desired height and covered with kiln shelves. Photo: author.

ing standard 9″ soaps (posts), set the kiln shelf and build the firing chamber up to the height you want. Here we are using a 23″-diameter shelf and building the chamber to a height of about 27″ from the floor. As you build up the chamber, be sure to integrate the joining of the firebox and firebox roof with the kiln chamber in a neat, tight fashion. For added insulating value, top off the firebox with earth. Leave plenty of flue opening for a draft and efficient combustion.

4–61
The first two courses of the firebox/ash pit and the first three courses of the firing chamber. Photo: author.

For less complicated design, build the kiln aboveground with simple brickwork. Arrange hard bricks on a concrete-block base for the floor of the kiln and firebox. Using standard 9″ insulating brick, lay the first course of bricks for a rectangular ash pit and firebox 36″ long (4 bricks) and 9″ wide (1 brick) interior dimensions. The interior dimensions of the firing chamber are 18″ square, set outside the firebox $\frac{1}{2}$ brick, making the entire kiln $58\frac{1}{2}$″ long. (Fig. 4–61) Three courses of brick form the ash pit. Note how a course is set in slightly to support the bricks used to hold the wood. (Fig. 4–62) You may substitute iron bars or some sort of grate if you wish. After two more courses, the firebox can be topped with bricks, spanning tile, or kiln shelves. Set the kiln shelf in the firing chamber level with the top of the firebox and continue to build up the chamber to the height you want. Use a lid of your choice. This kiln can function either as a top-loader or, with some slight modification, a front-loader.

4–62
View into the firebox showing the construction of the brick grating. The hard bricks used for the grate are called #1 splits and measure 9″ × $4\frac{1}{2}$″ × $1\frac{1}{4}$″. Photo: author.

4–63
The completed wood kiln with one shelf over the firebox removed. The kiln could be easily converted to a front-loader by incorporating an opening into the side of the chamber and making a door with individual bricks or with wire mesh lined with fiber. Photo: author.

Building a Coal-Fired Saggar Kiln

A brief mention of the coal-fired kiln is in order if for no other reason than to pay homage to tradition. Coal or charcoal may have been the fuel Chojiro used to fire his ware, but we cannot know for sure. Today, coal is rarely used by the raku potter. However, the fact is that a coal-fired raku kiln is easy to build, easy to fire, and requires no electricity, gas tanks, hoses, or burners.

To effectively use coal as a fuel, the ware must be isolated from the fuel through the use of a saggar. (More on saggars below.) As you can see in Figure 4–64, the coal kiln is little more than a chamber enclosing the saggar and fuel. It is not critical whether the chamber is cylindrical or cube shaped. More important is the tightness of construction, which is necessary for efficient heat retention. Harriet Brisson, who has had considerable experience with charcoal firing, provided the drawings and photos reproduced here. She reports excellent results using a soft brick, fiber, or the castable chamber in Figure 4–65. (Harriet's firing techniques will be discussed in Chapter 6.) If you build your chamber with brick, then for efficiency, make the chamber cube shaped. The fiber chamber is simply a wire cylinder, similar to our fiber kiln, but open at the top and bottom. Wire mesh also lines, but is not attached to the inside, to protect the fiber from the abrasion of the coal as it burns and settles.

Whether you use brick or fiber, you should have 4–6″ of space between the inside wall of the chamber and the saggar to allow plenty of room for the fuel to collect and burn. You also need to have 4–6″ of space between the top of the saggar and the top of the chamber. Note the air holes at the bottom of the chamber and how the saggar is set up on bricks to allow for sufficient draft, which is crucial to combustion. (Figs. 4–68 and 4–69) A lid fitted on top of the chamber with a flue cut into it will also act to increase draft and thus temperature. Use whatever lid you wish.

The saggar also has a lid, which can be treated as a tool for firing. Since the

4–64
A coal-fired brick saggar kiln. The lid and plug of the saggar have been removed to expose the pot in the saggar. A vacuum cleaner provides forced air to raise the temperature more rapidly. Photo: Harriet Brisson.

fuel goes no higher than the top of the saggar, the lid does not isolate the fuel from the ware. In this case, it acts to isolate the atmosphere in the saggar from that of the chamber. A lid is a necessity if you will want to saturate the saggar with material to create intense reduction effects within it. If not, you may wish to take advantage of the unavoidable reducing atmosphere created by using coal as your fuel. At any rate, the saggar must have a peep hole for viewing the ware, and if it does have a lid, it must be easily removable for access to the ware.

4–65
A saggar kiln made from castable mix. Note the hardwood charcoal around the saggar. Photo: Harriet Brisson.

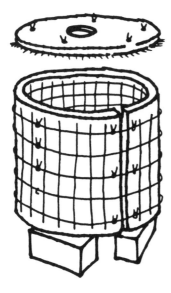

4–66

A fiber saggar kiln. The construction is identical to the expanded-metal fiber kiln except for the top. Wire mesh lines the inside as well and is held in place by the expansion of the mesh cylinder against the inside of the chamber. Drawing: Harriet Brisson.

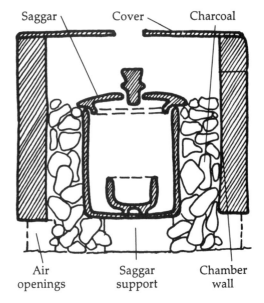

4–67

Cross section of the saggar and kiln. Drawing: Harriet Brisson.

4–68

A saggar set up on bricks and the first course of the chamber. Courtesy: Harriet Brisson.

For fuel, you can use coal, hardwood lump charcoal, or hardwood briquettes. The charcoal briquettes for barbecuing do not provide enough heat output and are polluting as well. (Refer back to the section on fuels for more detailed information on coal and charcoal.) Because the coal-fired saggar kiln is simple to make, it is certainly worth your effort to build one and experiment.

On the subject of saggars, let me mention that you can use a saggar in any type of kiln whenever you want to isolate your ware from direct contact with the fuel or flames. It is true that using a kiln shelf that fits tightly against the kiln walls does the job effectively, except in the case where the fuel surrounds the ware, as in the example above. Saggars are useful when you want to saturate the atmo-

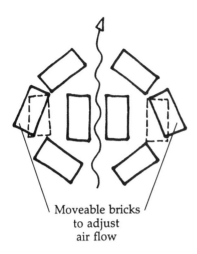

4–69

Top view of the brick arrangement showing the allowance for natural draft. Courtesy: Harriet Brisson.

sphere around the pots with a concentrated reduction. Using a saggar in this way is more common for high-fire techniques where you might load up a saggar with organic material to achieve a certain kind of reduction effect, but its use in raku has been documented and is definitely

worth experimenting with. (The creative use of saggars will be discussed in Chapter 8.)

Although the best are usually slab-built out of a raku-type clay (that is, a clay that is highly resistant to heat shock), saggars can be thrown as well. Even so, many potters will wrap the completed saggar with wire to keep it together in the event it should crack. Slab-building offers a structure that is generally more thermal resistant than a thrown form.

The lid of the saggar must be easily removable, and you must have a peep hole with a removable plug for viewing the pots during the firing cycle.

Chuck Hindes, who has done considerable work with cone 9–10 saggar firing, offers the following clay-body formulas:

Behren's Saggar Formula

Plastic fireclay	40
Calcined fireclay	30
Grog	28
Bentonite	2

4–70

Drawing of a thrown (left) and two hand-built saggars. The two grooves in the thrown saggar accommodate a wire wrap. Harriet punctures her saggars to allow the heavy carbon atmosphere of the burning charcoal access to the ware. Courtesy: Harriet Brisson.

Cardew Saggar Formula   (Hindes's Variation)

Grog	50	40
China clay	40	20
Bonding clay	10	
Ball clay		20
Talc		20

Hindes's Saggar Formula

Fireclay	2 parts by volume (e.g., 5-gallon bucket)
Ball clay	1
Ground course soft brick	1
Course saw-dust	2

4–71

Ronda Liskey with her dual-pad raku kiln. The fiber-lined expanded-metal firing chamber and the 22–gauge-metal reduction can swing from one brick pad to the other, allowing postfiring reduction to occur in place and eliminating the need to lift pots out of the kiln. When a smoking phase is completed and the pots are removed, a fresh batch can be loaded awaiting the lowering of the firing chamber. Photo: Raymond Kopen.

Reduction can 22g. sheet metal

2″ D × 14′ steel poles

50 lb. counter weight

Metal swivel connector

4″ × 4″ post 5′ h

3½′ h

3′ D

4′ Rebar as guide poles

¾″ × 13g. expanded metal

3½′ h

3′ D

26″ D shelf

Bisque the saggar to maintain its thermal qualities and expect it to last only several firings at best.

Brisson Saggar Formula

Fireclay	75
Grog	20
Talc	5

Bisque fire to cone 09.

Protecting a Kiln from the Elements

You will need to protect your kiln from the elements, particularly rain and snow,

4–72
A simple kiln cover made from a tarp and duct tape.

4–73
A kiln cover constructed of corrugated metal roofing on a wood frame. Photo: author.

if you want the kiln to outlast the current popular rock music. A little rain won't hurt (except in the case of a fiber kiln), but continuous exposure is harmful. The simplest way to protect your kiln is to cover it with a tarp after it has cooled down. Inexpensive waterproof tarps are available at hardware stores. A tarp can be unwieldly, though, and difficult to secure around the kiln. So, instead, custom-fit a cover for your kiln using tarp as the material. Cut the tarp to the appropriate length to fit around the kiln, leaving some extra space for burners and bricks. Attach the ends with duct tape or sew it with a sewing machine. Cut another piece for the cover and attach that. The disadvantage of using a tarp is that you must wait until the kiln is cool before you cover it. That often means coming back later that night. More often than not, I have been too lazy, or forgot, and not until it began to rain did I remember.

If you are very ambitious, you may want to build a roof over your kilns. A freestanding wood structure topped with corrugated metal roofing is perfectly adequate. Leave plenty of space around the kiln to allow the heat to dissipate and for unencumbered movement. If you cannot find corrugated metal roofing at your local building supply store, try a farm supply or feed store such as Agway.

Health and Safety

Chapter 5

Before dealing with what is undoubtedly the most dangerous aspect of the raku technique, the firing process, let's discuss health and safety practices. Throughout this book I have made reference to specific health and safety issues—for example, the elimination of lead from your materials list, protecting yourself when working with refractory fiber and brick, and safety practices when working around gas. A few other important precautions are to wear eye protection when peering into the kiln and to wear gloves, a mask, and protective clothing during the raku process. While I'm not about to break new ground here on the health and safety front, I cannot stress safety too much. Too many people suffer from the "It won't happen to me" syndrome. Potters, whether professional, hobby, or student, must realize that the materials, equipment, and surroundings they deal with regularly have the potential to cause, at the least, immediate short-term injury (burns, strains, irritation) and at the worst, chronic physiological conditions.

Much has been written over the past ten years on health and safety in the arts, and much of this information has even been added to art school curriculums so that "the future artists of America" will learn to be careful and avoid unnecessary risks. Yet it is still common to see even recent graduates not using eye protection, smoking in their studios (or smoking at all for that matter), sweeping their workplaces, or engaging in a variety of equally dangerous practices. The grave consequences of an irresponsible attitude toward "safe potting" warrants a reminder of some general studio practices, as well as safety issues as they relate specifically to the raku technique.

Safe Studio Practices

In fifteen years of setting up and operating my own studio as well as teaching in schools, I've learned a great deal about organization and safety in the studio. The first step in this process is to lay out your workspace in a logical manner. It doesn't matter whether you have only a small space in your basement or a spacious studio, safety begins here. I don't want to discuss how to design a space for maximum efficiency and production but rather to offer some tips on how to reduce the likelihood of tripping over your own pots. Giving yourself generous table tops, countertops, and shelves allows you to keep things off the floor. Keep stairways and doorways clear. The first comment I hear from visitors upon entering my studio, *The Potters Shop*, for the first time is, "I've never seen so many shelves!"

One of your goals it to lay out spaces that require the least amount of reaching for supplies and tools. Try to organize your clay and materials storage areas close to outside entrances or loading docks. (Your back will thank you!) Another goal is ventilation. Every studio requires ventilation, whether general or task-specific. General ventilation means the air in the studio overall or in a particular room; task-specific ventilation means air brushing, sanding, or melting wax (for wax emulsion.) For a complete treatment of ventilation in your studio, read *Ventilation* by Nancy Clark. (See the Bibliography.)

Never dry-sweep your studio. Instead, wet-clean or use an appropriate HEPA filter-equipped vacuum cleaner, such as a Nilfisk. *Never, under any circumstances, use a home vacuum cleaner or Shop-Vac.* The filter systems are not designed to trap the fine particle-size dust that potters produce. Using a Shop-Vac in our environment will most certainly clog and ruin its motor. More significant, though, is that it will simply recirculate the air with silica and whatever else you happen to be cleaning up. Don't let an overzealous salesperson convince you otherwise. Stay away from sweeping compounds as well. Their use

5–1
Part of the main work area at The Potters Shop.

will lessen the airborne particles but will not eliminate them.

Raku and Personal Safety

Every step along the way, the raku technique, particularly the firing process, exposes the potter to risk of injury. Before discussing the more obviously dangerous aspects of doing raku, let me say another word about the functional use of raku ware.

Uncertainty often arises regarding the functional use of raku ware, no doubt because traditionally raku ware has been associated with the Japanese tea ceremony. Historically, we can attribute raku's use in the ceremony to a lack of knowledge regarding the potential harmful effects of lead toxicity and fired glaze solubility. In addition, the tea ceremony, being a ritual, was not an everyday practice, and raku ware was only one of several types of ware used. So exposure to health risks during the ceremony were diminished.

Today, while I don't recommend its use, non-lead-glazed raku ware is considered by some to be safe, depending on the nature of the foods or liquids used, if the glaze meets chemical-release standards, and, again, if the ware is used infrequently. Nevertheless, I repeat my previous advice: regard raku ware of all types as *decorative* and do not use it for food or drink.

In the section on kiln placement, I stressed the importance of eliminating physical obstacles around the kiln. I discussed designing the kiln so the chamber is easily accessible with a minimum of awkward, heavy lifting. Both approaches are simple to achieve and are effective measures toward safe raku firing. Also in respect to kiln placement is the fact that

while gas-fired kilns of all types are routinely housed indoors, including in basements, they are fueled by natural gas only. Those fueled by propane should always be located outdoors. Of course electric and oil-fired kilns are suitable for indoor placement as well.

Another important consideration is simple but perhaps not so obvious. As I was writing this chapter, I received some literature advertising a kiln (the manufacturer will remain nameless). The description of the kiln included the following:

> The top 18″ of the kiln can be easily elevated by the turn of a hand winch. This allows easy access to the firing chamber while trapping the heat in the kiln and away from the operator, thus eliminating the need for expensive protective clothing while Rakuing.

"Eliminating the need for expensive protective clothing" is irresponsible and extremely dangerous. No raku kiln, no matter how it is designed, will trap the heat in the kiln away from the operator when it is opened to expose the ware. *Always* wear appropriate clothing! Wear long pants and foot coverings. Those pots, tongs, and reduction containers are hot, and even your shirt, jeans, and sneakers will give you some time to react if you come in contact with a hot object. If you have long hair, tie it back to keep it out of the kiln and out of the way of flames from reduction material. Sounds crazy? Don't be so sure. And while we are on the subject of hair, if you're not careful, arm hair, facial hair, eyebrows, and even eyelashes can easily be singed from close contact with the heat from the kiln. No, you don't need to wear a flame-retardant race car driver's suit— just a few intelligent articles of clothing will suffice.

The single most important piece of protective wear is a pair of gloves. For high heat exposure, such as removing pots from the kiln or any close contact with the kiln or pots, I suggest Kevlar gloves that pull up over your wrists. Gloves come in three or four different lengths, and I often use 23″ gloves that come up to my biceps. These gloves are either lined with cotton or wool or unlined. The lined glove affords slightly more protection, although they are warm in the summer. Kevlar is more durable than the traditional asbestos gloves and are just as resistant to heat, and at least as protective without adding the danger of asbestos exposure. As far as I know, asbestos gloves are no longer manufactured, but even if you have an old pair, don't use them. Spend the money—and they are expensive—and buy new, safe Kevlar gloves.

Even though Kevlar gloves are heavy in weight and formidable looking, they are not designed for rough treatment, nor should they be allowed to get wet. For moderate heat conditions, such as handling reduction containers, applying reduction materials, and removing warm

pots after reduction, heavy leather work gloves or welding or fireplace gloves will suffice. Ah ha! you say. Why not combine the refractory protection of Kevlar with the durability of leather? It's already been done, and my advice is to not use leather-palm Kevlar gloves. When the leather is exposed consistently to high heat, it becomes stiff. Use Kevlar gloves for high heat and leather gloves for everything else.

Face and eye protection are crucial to your safety in the studio. Whenever you look into the kiln, you should protect your eyes by wearing appropriate lenses. The safety standard for looking into kilns is a C-4 lens. For protection from the heat of the kiln while raku firing, wear a lightweight mask of clear plastic, the kind designed for protection from flying particles during grinding. Use the mask by *wearing* it! If you hold it up in front of the flue at arm's length while looking through it, as I have seen some potters do, the mask will melt and deform.

Do I practice what I preach? For the

5–2
Kevlar gloves for optimum heat protection (left) *and leather gloves for general use around the raku site* (right). *The gloves in the center are 23″ long. Kevlar sleeves can be used in combination with gloves.*

5–3
A general shop face mask affords good protection when working in close proximity to the heat of the kiln.

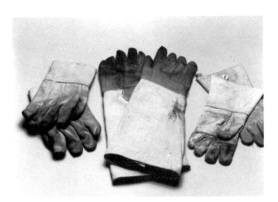

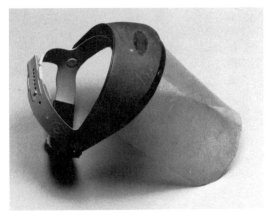

most part, yes, but let me say something about being "practical" in one's safety measures versus going strictly by the book. Clothing, for instance, is crucial, and while it is absolutely safer to wear long pants and a long-sleeve shirt, if I am firing small pieces in 80-degree weather, I must admit I sometimes wear shorts and a short-sleeve shirt. Likewise, if I am maintaining a tong-length distance from the kiln chamber, most likely I will not be wearing a face protector. And if I can spy into the chamber from a safe distance, four feet or so, I may not be wearing eye protection.

My alertness to safety is always at its peak when I'm giving a workshop or when other people are nearby. Then I am most conservative regarding safety because accidents are more likely to happen when the studio or workspace is crowded and casual. Am I practicing safe raku firing? Yes, I am, and I raise these points to illustrate where experience can temper overcautiousness. For example, a common malady in beginning raku firing is pots breaking during the heating cycle. If you look into the kiln from close range and a pot blows up, you can be on the receiving end of a shard flying out of the flue or peep hole. As an experienced raku potter, the likelihood of that happening to me is low—not because I am impervious to flying shards, but because my pots aren't likely to explode in the kiln. Never let down your guard concerning safety. Always err on the side of caution and over-protect yourself. At a recent workshop I conducted, a participant was outfitted in a full-length leather suit! More power to her.

Make it a habit to inspect your equipment prior to every firing. Examine your tongs, checking the bolt or rivet for looseness or weakness where they pivot. Check your entire burner system for leaks or cor-

rosion, and check the integrity of the hose. Check the handles on your lid or kiln for tightness and strength. The same goes for the lid itself and door hinges. Scrutinize your gloves for rips, tears, and holes.

Choreograph your firings. Even if you are a one-person operation, plan your moves and have everything in order before you start. If you have assistance, make sure each person has a designated role. In the often frenzied cacophony of removing pots from the kiln, reaching for tools, and applying reduction material, danger abounds. It is easy to swing around with pot on tong aiming for your barrel only to have your once-clear path obstructed by your co-rakuist's leg. Ouch!

If you are new to raku, make some trial runs. Reach into a cold kiln and pull out some bisque pots typical of the ones you will be firing. Observe how much space you will need around you and find a convenient place for your reduction material and containers. Too many details, you say? No need to plan out so many little things? You can never do too much preparation! Several times at least (and I

5–4
A careful inspection of your equipment prior to firing will protect against easily avoidable accidents.

should be embarrassed to admit it), I stood with a pot hot from the kiln with either all my reduction barrels full or the piece too large for the nearest container. This scenario is not as unlikely as it may seem.

Any firing against the backdrop of a dark sky is dramatic and exciting. However, always take extreme caution when firing at night. The reduced visibility can increase the chance of accidents. Even if the site is well lighted, shadows from the lights will make it difficult to see. Keep your number of participants to a minimum, maintain careful control over each person's activity, and be acutely aware of all the activity going on.

Although I previously stressed (and will stress again later) various safety practices with regard to your gas supply, burner system, and kiln, some of them bear repeating here. Keep the area clear of combustible materials, such as leaves or any stray reduction materials that might be left over from a previous firing. The same goes for low hanging branches and other landscaping features. (These, of course, are things you should have thought about when you built your kiln!) Flying sparks or a dropped pot could result in an impromptu open-pit barbecue. If you unload your kiln by removing the lid altogether, be sure you place it on a cement block or brick pad, thereby preventing the hot lid from coming in contact with grass or material that could ignite. Keep observers at a safe distance and tell them beforehand to resist the temptation to "help" you out during the firing if it seems that you need help. I could go on dissecting each detail for safety issues, but it all comes down to proceeding with a slow, deliberate, safety-conscious attitude. With this approach, together with the other specific points mentioned here, you can't go wrong.

Along with safety, let me mention building codes, open burning codes, Morse codes, and the litany of codes applicable to eating, breathing, and sleeping. Local town ordinances and building codes are designed with the safety of people in

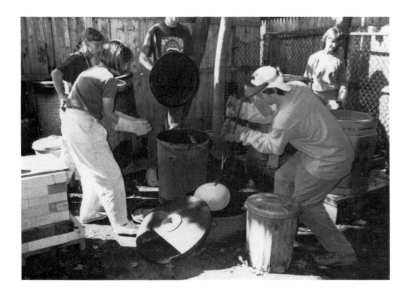

5–5
The excitement and frenzy of a firing can easily lead to accidents. Participants must know what their place and responsibilities are. Photo: author.

mind (although they often seem like a sadist's idea of an obstacle course). Likewise, your raku facility, whether it's a small electric kiln, one garbage can, or a veritable raku city, should be designed without taking any safety shortcuts. Obviously, the installation of natural gas lines or the setting up of a 500-gallon propane tank should be professionally inspected and approved. Problems arise, however, when you try to explain just what a raku kiln is, or what postfiring reduction is, to the powers that be in order to get official permission to operate. Having no firsthand experience with kilns, these powers often are not receptive to being educated. What should you do? I'm afraid I must leave that to your own good conscience. Situations, locations, and various circumstances will dictate the proper course of action. Do you live in a rural area with not another house in sight or do you live in a densely populated neighborhood? Are there other potters in your area with kilns? What did they do? Is there a school with kilns nearby? Does the fire chief live three houses down the street from you? These are not easy issues to deal with, but you should approach them up front with only the highest regard for your safety and the safety of your surroundings.

Above all, think clearly, use common sense, and let caution govern all situations. Never carelessly take anything for granted. Follow my advice and soon you will strike a balance between concentrating on your pottery and being attentive to safety.

The Firing Process

When all this has been done, prayers are offered to God with the whole heart, ever thanking Him for all that He gives us. Fire is taken, having an eye however to the state of the moon, for this is of the greatest importance, and I have heard from those who are old in the art and of some experience that, if the firing happens to take place at the waning of the moon, the fire lacks brightness in the same manner as the moon its splendour. In doing this, therefore, pay attention to it, especially when it is in the rainy signs, which would be very perilous and must be allowed to pass over, remembering always to do all the things in the name of Christ Jesus.

—Cipriano Piccolpasso,
The Three Books of the Potters Art

Chapter 6

Our feelings toward the firing of our ware will no doubt be more earthbound and we will feel more in control than our friend Cipriano. Nonetheless, if there is a heart and soul of the raku technique it is the firing process. Our pots, no matter how beautiful they seem to us, are lifeless until they emerge from the kiln. This is where all of our preparations—technical, mental, and aesthetic—come together. Firing is the proof of the pudding and the rope that ties it all together. Even in the raku firing process, which is simple and relatively straightforward, there are many variables that can both work against us and that we can use to our advantage.

Initial Preparation

You have located your kiln in the appropriate place and have anticipated and solved all the preliminary problems. You have tested the burners and, yes, they ignite and the kiln heats up. You are off to a good start. Below is a preparation checklist. Whatever details that might seem to be missing from the checklist will be discussed as each step of the raku process unfolds. Planning for the firing should include the following;

- If you are using propane, wood, or coal, check that you have an adequate supply for your planned firings.
- Assemble the correct number and size of reduction containers and arrange these containers for easy access as well as clear movement around the kiln.
- Place your reduction material at a safe distance from the kiln yet within easy reach for quick access during the postfiring process.
- Will you need assistance during any part of the firing? For instance, lifting the lid, applying reduction materials, or turning off the fuel supply. If so, make sure your helpers, whether in a workshop situation or for your own firing, know what their jobs and responsibilities are.
- Arrange for a constant water source for emergency situations as well as for cooling and washing your pots.

- Are the kiln and firing site safe and secure from onlookers?
- Provide safe, clear avenues for complete unencumbered movement around the kiln.
- If you are firing multiple loads, have the next batch of pots preheated and situated for easy loading into the kiln.

Having an adequate fuel supply on hand is an absolute must. For propane, make sure you start your firings with full tanks of gas. A 25- or 50-pound bag of charcoal should be enough for one firing, but have 50 or even 100 pounds for multiple firings. Planning for a wood firing is difficult the first time. The amount of fuel you use will depend on the type of wood, the size of the pieces of wood, and your rate of stoking. It's not a bad idea to have $\frac{1}{4}$ to $\frac{1}{2}$ cord [32–64 cubic feet] of wood on hand.

Reduction materials and containers may have piqued your curiosity. Reduction materials will be discussed in the section on postfiring, but containers deserve

6–1
Galvanized cans in a variety of sizes make excellent reduction containers.

some mention now. Galvanized buckets and garbage cans with matching lids are the most common containers used in raku and in fact are ideal for most applications. They meet all three basic needs: they are available in various sizes to accommodate your ware, are fire- and heat-resistant, and their lids fit snugly, making an effectively airtight chamber. Galvanized cans in 5-, 10-, 20-, and 30-gallon sizes, as well as tubs, are available in hardware stores and at home centers. Long galvanized troughs are available at farm supply stores and perhaps at hardware stores that will special-order products. Galvanized cans last a reasonably long time, especially if they are stored out of the rain. Their one potential disadvantage is that they offer little in the way of insulating value, thus your pots will cool rather quickly. With large or otherwise sensitive work, this could be a problem. To slow down the cooling of his ware, Wayne Higby uses a wooden box insulated with fiber and lined with thin sheet metal. (Fig. 6–2)

You can often find wonderful con-tainers, including larger ones, by checking the Yellow Pages under "Barrels" or "Cans." Manufacturers and distributors frequently have "seconds" and used goods available at reasonable prices. Resourceful potters have made use of discarded refrigerators and freezers (after removing the plastic interiors), as well as all kinds of steel drums and barrels.

The most basic enclosure, and one that might be the only possibility if your work is large, is a hole dug in the ground covered with a steel lid, barrel, or earth. Susan and Steven Kemenyffy use this method for their grand pieces. Any container is fair game as long as you can adapt it to your particular needs and requirements. Be sure to remove any plastic parts from containers you will use as reduction enclosures.

The reasons for paying attention to these details of planning and other nuances of your particular firing style and needs will become absolutely clear as the firing proceeds. However, as is true with many things, often we need to make some

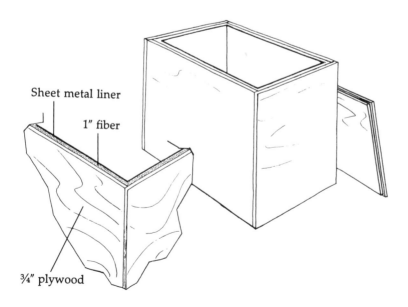

Sheet metal liner

1" fiber

¾" plywood

6–2
A wooden reduction container after a design by Wayne Higby. The cover is soaked with water shortly before use.

initial mistakes before we realize the importance of planning and organization.

Stacking the Kiln

So you've been stacking and firing kilns for years and are ready to skip this part and rely on your own expertise. Back up. It's true that stacking a kiln efficiently is a skill that comes with experience, but efficiency is only one of several aspects important in stacking for raku firing. Your primary concerns in raku are to isolate your ware as much as possible from the flames of the burner (unless you choose to ignore this for some aesthetic reason), to not block efficient air and fuel flow in the kiln, and to be able to remove the pots from the kiln with the greatest of ease.

Flames are ever present in fuel-fired kilns. The point is to try to keep direct flames from hitting the pots. Direct contact with flames is a major cause of breakage early in the firing. If you have properly designed your burner port so that it is under the kiln shelf, you shouldn't have a problem. Don't worry too much about flames that travel up the side of the kiln and hug the wall.

Before going any further, coat your kiln shelf with a good layer of kiln wash. Glaze drips are inevitable, especially early in your raku career. However, there is no need to sacrifice a glaze-free, smooth shelf surface because you are inexperienced with the raku technique. Mistreated shelves quickly become bumpy with globs of glaze that will stick to the bottoms of the ware and inhibit efficient stacking of the kiln. Carelessly treated shelves are also prone to premature cracking. Make it a habit to scrape and kiln-wash your shelves before each firing session and you won't have to replace them every few firings.

Achieving control over your glazes will come in time, but, meanwhile, preserve your equipment!

Kiln Wash

EPK [Kaolin]	2 parts
Flint	2 parts
Alumina hydrate	1 part

Mix by volume measurement (cup, scoop) to a creamy consistency and apply two coats with a wide brush.

Ware must be arranged in the kiln in a way that will facilitate its removal. If you are purposely firing glazes that mature at different temperatures, you must be able to remove the cooler maturing glazed ware easily without disturbing the rest of the kiln load. In stacking conventional kilns, the goal is to load the ware as efficiently as possible and at the same time fit in as many pots as possible. This is not always important in a raku firing. If the pots fit together one way when placed in the kiln, they must come out the opposite way, so make a note of this before you fumble your way through to remove your work.

Remember that speed is very important in removing your pots. Blundering your way through the removal step can cause accidents and result in breakage and less than perfect firing results. Plates and other flat pieces can be loaded standing up on their edges, which usually makes them easy to grab with tongs. A cautionary note, however: Ware loaded in this manner has a high likelihood of warping. The problem with loading plates or other wide forms right-side up is twofold: First, they can take up an exorbitant amount of space in the kiln; second, you don't want a wide form blocking your flue and cutting off your draft. I have often seen situations where a bowl or plate is stacked on top of

6–3
A tightly stacked front-loader. Ware is stacked right up to the door, including on the floor of the kiln.

another piece to save space, but it is directly under the flue opening, blocking the air flow and causing a very slow or stagnating firing.

Can ware be touching in a raku firing? Since you are too embarrassed to ask a question with such an unmistakably clear and unequivocal answer, I asked it for you. Sure, they can be touching. Again, your decision to have pots touching rests on your aesthetic expectations and how much work you feel compelled to load into the kiln at once. Often, especially in workshop situations, where there always seems to be more work than could ever be fired, I load ware foot to rim and all over each other. Generally, if your pieces are touching side to side, it is likely that given

quick removal from the kiln there will either be no evidence that they were touching or the glazes may show colors or effects from another piece. Usually the point of contact will smooth out after the pots are separated and cool down.

Certainly if a glazed area was in contact with an unglazed area, the results will be more obvious. When pots are stacked rim to foot, the otherwise unglazed foot will become glazed with whatever it was resting on. In the case of unglazed surfaces coming in contact, there are usually no effects. The risk of stacking your work in this way is that if you don't remove your pots fast enough, as they cool they will stick together in the kiln. The only way to "unstick" these pots is to leave them in the kiln, reheat, and then remove them when the glaze has melted again. No harm done. A word of caution: If glazed pots have begun to stick to each other, as you pull them from the kiln a thin thread of hot glaze can be created similar to melted cheese coming off a pizza as you take a slice from the pie. This can be dangerous because it will harden quickly, and if *you* should come in contact with it, you could be cut or burned or both. Be careful!

Kiln furniture can certainly be useful for stacking. Front-loading kilns with shelves give you more stacking efficiency. In the case of top-loaders, shelves are an obstacle and a nuisance. Having to reach down into the kiln and under a half shelf is an exercise in trying to make a rigid object (tongs) flexible. The only furniture I use in my top-loaders are bricks to raise the level of the work higher simply to bring it closer to the top of the kiln or to allow it to clear or fit better between another pot. I have also positioned a shelf above a piece with a pot stacked on it if I determined that removing the shelf with tongs to expose the pot below would be quick and easy. The exception to the use of shelves in a top-loader is the cylindrical fiber kiln, where the entire chambers lifts off to expose the ware. (Fig. 6–4) Problems that arise here involve the careful raising and lowering of the kiln to safely clear the edges of the shelves—a skillful task.

When stacking an electric kiln for raku firing, aside from stacking to facilitate easy removal of the ware, there are two other primary concerns:

1. If you use a top-loader, stack your ware so that the tallest piece is within 1–2″ of the top of the kiln. To do this you will need to use a kiln shelf,

6–4

Andrew Berends's fiber-lined drum kiln shows how shelves are used in this type of application. If the kiln should swing excessively while being lifted off, the result could be disastrous! Courtesy Andrew Berends.

which eliminates the need to reach deep into the kiln, having to open the lid of the kiln very wide, or having to get too close to the kiln itself. For a front-loader, stack as close to the front of the kiln as possible for the same reasons.

2. Keep your pieces 1–2″ from the sides of the kiln. This will help avoid touching the brick with your tongs and help keep glaze drips off the walls of the kiln.

The Firing Cycle

Management of the firing cycle differs slightly depending on type of fuel used. Electricity requires the least tending and in fact essentially no tending at all up to the point of maturity. Gas requires careful (but minimal) attention, while wood and coal demand continual supervision. While our discussion will focus primarily on gas systems, I will mention electricity, wood, and coal whenever appropriate.

Before describing the actual cycle, let's begin with the correct assembly and attachment of the burner system. Since natural gas fittings require professional installation, we will assume that has been completed. If you are using a commercial propane burner system, or if your burner system came with your kiln, then follow the instructions supplied for attaching any necessary fittings. If when you purchase your burner, hoses, and fittings you have the option of having them assembled for you, do take advantage of this. When the assembly comes to you pressure-tested and ready to use, it is worth the extra

cost. If you do not have directions on how to fit the system to your tank, follow these guidelines:

- Propane fittings are threaded opposite to conventional plumbing or screw fittings, meaning that to tighten you turn *counterclockwise* and to loosen you turn *clockwise*. Knowing this will prevent a nervous breakdown as you try to attach your system to your tank.
- Most fittings to propane tanks can be hand-tightened without needing to use a wrench to tighten. The male portion of the fitting is fitted with a rubber "O" ring that acts as a gasket. If you have a different type, a wrench may be necessary.
- Check all connections for leaks with a soapy water solution before ignition.

Some potters insist on preheating the kiln *before* stacking the first load. I don't see any reason to do this, thus my first load is always fired from a cold kiln. This gives you the opportunity to stack your first load leisurely and carefully and to use the first load to fire your larger, more delicate pieces that may be prone to breakage. For an electric kiln, load your pots, turn the kiln on high, and come back later in the chapter when I talk about recognizing glaze melt, maturity, soaking, underfiring, and overfiring. The firing will take 2–3 hours depending on the size of the kiln and the condition of the coils.

Several techniques can be used to light the burner or, in the case of wood or coal, the fuel. For a venturi burner system with propane, you can use a welder's sparker, a match, or one of those newfangled butane lighters that have a long tip designed for lighting barbecues. I have never gotten comfortable using a sparker. I don't like having to put my hand so close to the flame, and every time it lights, no matter how well prepared I am, I always jump! My preferred method is to light the end of a few sheets of rolled-up newspaper.

"Propane is heavier than air." We have all heard this ominous warning, but just what does it mean in real life? It means that when propane is released into the air as a gas it falls to the ground. As it falls, it doesn't dissipate as rapidly as other gases. This is why propane tanks should never be used or stored indoors, especially below ground. In the case of our kiln, the practical application of this knowledge is concerned with lighting our burner safely and efficiently. Open the primary air control and flue, have your sparker or lighted match in hand, turn on the gas until you can hear it flow, and light the burner by placing the match in front of the burner head. Do this with the burner in place. If the gas flow is too weak, it won't light. If it doesn't light within about three seconds, shut off the gas and try again after waiting a minute or so. This gives the gas that has entered the kiln time to escape. You shouldn't have any trouble if you use the newspaper tech-

6–6
A lit sheet of rolled-up newspaper is a safe way to light your burner.

nique. If you are using a sparker, you may have to practice.

Igniting wood and coal is a bit trickier than gas. There is no convenient valve to use to turn up the power. Your own manipulation of the fuel becomes the "valve." As I said earlier, wood firings begin with larger pieces of wood. Place a layer of newspaper, wood shavings, excelsior, twigs, or any other kindling on the grates of the firebox. On top of this place some larger pieces of wood, 4"–5" in diameter or greater. Light the kindling, allowing it to ignite the wood. Use these and other large pieces of wood to begin the firing, preheating the chamber and your ware. As the ware and chamber increase in temperature, gradually decrease the size of the wood. Wood pieces 1" in diameter and smaller are used at the height of the firing.

Coal should be lit in the same manner if you are using the coal on grates as in a wood kiln. In a saggar kiln, place the kindling in the chamber with a layer of coals over it. Light the kindling and, when the coals have begun to ashen, pour in more charcoal to the top of the saggar. Continue adding more charcoal as the firing progresses and the coals burn away.

Unless I am in a workshop situation or am behind in my production schedule, I fire single loads of raku. That is, I do not fire one load while preheating the next to be loaded into the kiln and subsequently fired. My work is too large to preheat safely. Then again, I do have four kilns that I can fire simultaneously, thus obviating the need to do multiple loads.

My firings take one to three hours depending on the size of the work. You will need to experiment if fast firing is your goal. Raku can be fired in cycles as short as 15 or 20 minutes (I have even witnessed 10-minute firings), but understand that most breakage occurs when going from cold to hot (the heating stage), not from hot to cold (the cooling stage). Your firing cycles will depend on the clay body, your preheating success, and the initial temperature advance once the ware has been placed in the chamber. (More on preheating and fast-firing techniques later.) If you are just starting out, be conservative and fire slowly until you gain some experience in recognizing appropriate temperature rise.

Controlling Combustion and Temperature Rise

Controlling the temperature in your kiln is a combined function of gas flow or stoking, primary and secondary air, and flue and wind—all the factors discussed earlier in relation to combustion theory. Probably the most difficult concept to master is the relationship of air to temperature rise. Remember when we learned in elementary

school science that a candle needs air to burn? That knowledge will come in handy here! Think of air in respect to your kiln as the fine-turning control is to your television set. As you adjust the control, the picture gets clearer until it is at it's optimum quality. As you continue to turn, the picture quality begins to deteriorate. In your kiln, insufficient air results in a yellow flame, resulting in a reduction atmosphere. As you "tune in" or increase your air, whether primary, secondary, or flue, the flame gets bluer, hotter, and more efficient. Continue to "tune" and too much air will result in a flame that is blue but not hot. If you want to lower the temperature in the kiln, turn down the gas and then adjust your air for an efficient blue flame.

Another confusing concept related to air and temperature rise is the adjustment of the damper or flue. The flue controls the power of the draft in the kiln—that is, how strong the air pull is. Assuming that you begin with the right flue size, generally the more open it is, the more draft; the more draft, the more air; the more air, the bluer and hotter the flame. When the flue is opened and you can feel the radiant heat, understand that while some heat is escaping, it must be this way! Resist the somewhat logical tendency to close off the flue in order to "keep in the heat," thinking that will cause the temperature to rise. It won't work!

Draft is also affected by the warmth of the kiln itself. On the first firing of the day, the kiln is cold and the draft will be weak. You will see flames in the kiln, and it will seem impossible to achieve a blue oxidizing flame at the burner tip. As the kiln heats up, the draft and your ability to control the kiln will improve. In extreme situations, a poor draft will cause flames to shoot out of the burner port. To avoid a fire hazard, build a brick enclosure (Fig. 6–7) or wall to enclose the flames temporarily. Remove the enclosure when the draft improves.

Let me reiterate the importance of not blocking the flue with your ware and not stacking any pots so close to the opening that they will be prevented from reaching temperature. A plate or wide form stacked directly under the flue opening will block the draft. Also, glazed pieces stacked near the flue, say within three inches of the top of the kiln, even if they don't inhibit the draft, may not reach maturity because that part of the chamber tends to be cooler than the rest of the kiln. Place unglazed ware or ware with lower maturing glazes there instead.

Because air is essential for efficient combustion, try to maximize your control of it. Wind, obviously a great source of air, offers you a free power burner system.

If possible, locate your kiln so any wind will blow toward the burner port, not against the opposite side of the kiln. Wind blowing this way or into the flue can have a negative effect on your control of the kiln by preventing an efficient draft. This can result in a cooling effect. The wind can also blow the flame back out of the burner port, which can be a fire hazard. To prevent this, build a brick shield to protect the flue from the wind (Fig. 6–8) as well as one to enclose the burner.

Weather conditions other than wind can negatively affect your firing. While larger kilns are easily affected by factors such as ambient temperature and barometric pressure, raku kilns, being small and often overpowered anyway, are generally unaffected. Firing an unprotected kiln in the rain is usually nothing more than uncomfortable. I am often asked if I fire in cold weather or when there is snow on the ground. I certainly do! Cold outside temperatures will cause your ware to cool

6–7

A simple brick enclosure will effectively enclose flames that may back out of the port as a result of temporary poor draft.

6–8

These bricks shield the flue from excessive wind.

6–9
A little snow or cold weather shouldn't discourage you from firing! Photo: author.

faster and inhibit preheating subsequent loads, conditions that vary in importance from one potter to another. Extreme cold will cause premature freeze-ups and pressure loss in propane tanks. The smaller the tank, the more likely the problem. Be sure to have hot water available to pour over the tank in the event of a freeze-up.

Snow presents a different problem. While the heat generated by the kiln will keep you warm while you tend it, this same heat will melt the snow around the kiln and could create a real mess depending on what the kiln and you are standing on. Dirt and grass will get muddy and slippery from the melting snow, creating a potentially dangerous situation in light of all the movement that takes place around the kiln during the unloading phase. A concrete slab or other hard surface will be less affected by wetness, but you must guarantee yourself sure footing.

The Firing Schedule

A good initial firing schedule is as follows: Light the burner and adjust the flame so that it is clearly audible. The volume of the burner is an accurate indicator of its intensity and power. Too soft a flame and you run the risk of extinguishing it. Begin with the burner head just inside the kiln. (Fig. 6–10) This lessens the chance of the flame being extinguished if you adjust it too low. The primary air control and the damper should be opened to the max. Remember that until your kiln is thoroughly hot, draft will be minimal and you may notice that the flame is yellow. At this stage, there is little you can do to eliminate flames in the chamber. This is normal and nothing to worry about. As the kiln heats up, the draft will improve and, if you have done everything correctly, you will have no trouble achieving a blue oxidizing flame. After 15 minutes pull the

6–10
Initially, when the draft is weak, the burner should be just inside the kiln.

burner out of the kiln so it is an inch or two away from the kiln (see Fig. 6–11) and turn up the gas until you notice a difference in the quality of the flame and loudness of the burner.

Continue to turn up the burner every 15 minutes until the glazed surfaces and the bare clay begin to take on a dark, gray quality. This indicates that the ware has *sintered*—that is, changed from a soft state that can still be slaked down with water to a hard, permanent state. (This appearance is not to be confused with the black carbon deposits associated with a reduction atmosphere early in the firing.) You will notice a change in the appearance of the glaze long before there is any melting of the glaze or a glow in the kiln. Once this darker quality is visible, it is usually safe to turn the burner up all the way. If you are not sure and prefer caution, then by

6–11

The burner at about the optimum distance from the kiln.

all means continue slowly. When the chamber begins to take on an orange glow (and sometimes even before), you will begin to notice glaze "meltage." We now move into the next phase of the firing cycle.

At this stage, adjusting the firing becomes more fine-tuned and somewhat critical. The issues here include firing the glazes so all the ware in the kiln matures at the same time, possible reduction effects, and soaking, to name a few.

Having the glazes reach simultaneous maturity is the climax of the firing. Acquiring this skill requires patience and comes with experience. Unlike conventional firing, where the relatively simple task of viewing melted cones signals the firing's end, the rapid firing, changing atmospheres, and the firing of multiple loads effectively rule out the use of cones in raku. Being one who welcomes variations in approaches, though, I wouldn't completely disregard their potential use. For example, cones could aid in the firing of a load of unglazed or matt-glazed ware from a cold kiln. Within the temperature range of raku, the color and brightness in the kiln still enables us to see the surfaces on our wares. With practice and careful perception, you will be able to recognize proper glaze melt.

As the kiln approaches firing temperature, the chamber will go from no color to a bright glowing orange. At the same time, the glazes evolve from a dry state through various degrees of melting. The first obvious change is when the glazes just begin to melt. Surfaces take on a living appearance, moving and changing almost second by second. I refer to this stage as the "ugly stage" because the glazes look truly *ugly*. There is the slightest degree of shininess, and the surface looks like it is about to separate from the pot, leaving areas void of glaze. As the temperature increases, these surfaces begin to smooth out and the glossiness intensifies. At this point, if you observe carefully, you can see small pimple-like eruptions and pinhole craters on a very shiny surface. What we are looking for now is a smooth, defect-free, shimmering, gloss-like effect on the surface of the ware. This final stage of melting has been likened to "the reflection of water on ice in the sunlight," and I find this to be an accurate, if not the most poetic, description. Resign yourself to the fact that there is no substitute for experience and seeing this for yourself. Depending on your rate of firing, the time between seeing the first signs of melting and maturity could be anywhere from 15 minutes to an hour. When viewing the work, try to spy *across* the surfaces rather than looking straight down at the glaze. Depending on the glaze, this maturing point may be within a very narrow temperature range or a very wide one. Only experience will tell.

If you allow the glaze to continue firing, overfiring will result, and you can observe vigorous boiling on the surface similar to the eruptions as the glaze was reaching temperature, except these pimples will not smooth out! Another interesting note on glaze maturity: If you are firing any copper matt wash, don't expect it to melt and look shiny like a conventional glaze. A copper matt wash will always look dry and underfired in the kiln. Don't use a pot with copper matt wash as your observation piece, that is, the piece you use to determine the readiness of the firing.

In storybooks, kilns fire perfectly evenly and all glazes mature at the same time. This doesn't often happen in real life. Most often the glazes closer to the bottom of the kiln will melt before those at the top, and you've got to do something about it. One effective means of evening out the temperature is to begin a moderate reduction to slow down the firing and increase the flow of gases and flame through the kiln. In addition to evening out the temperature in the kiln, this process will produce interesting reduction effects in your glazes. Simply close off the flue until you see a hint of flames coming out of it and the peep holes when you remove the plugs. You usually don't have to turn down the gas or adjust the primary air—the flue will do it all. It's also not neces-

6–12

Kiln during heavy reduction (exaggerated for the photo). Visible flames are always an indication of incomplete combustion, or reduction.

sary to have clouds of billowing smoke and flames ten feet long shooting out of the kiln.

Speaking of reduction, I have used the word throughout the book accompanied by various degrees of explanation. However, I don't want to take anything for granted. The first time I heard the term was when my college pottery teacher asked me to check the kiln to see that the reduction was going well. Being a first-year pottery student, this was the first time *I* had been asked to check the kiln, so I was feeling proud and important. The kiln was a mile away and I didn't realize until I got there that I hadn't the foggiest idea of what I was suppose to be looking for. Was the kiln shrinking, getting smaller during the firing? Was this what reduction meant?

Reduction means reducing the amount of oxygen to the fuel, thereby increasing the amount of carbon from the unburned fuel. This carbon reacts with various glaze materials by causing them to seek out oxygen for their chemical reactions other than the oxygen in the atmosphere. Reds, purples, and other reduction firing effects are the result. Reduction must be carried out for at least 15 minutes to have any appreciable aesthetic effects in raku. If you want to even out the kiln yet not have the result be reduction effects, then upon even maturity open up the flue for a minute or so and most if not all of the effect will be eliminated. Another quick note on reduction: Reduction during the firing is not to be confused with the *postfiring reduction* that is so characteristic of Western raku and that I will explore later.

A final helpful technique in realizing proper glaze melt is to allow a period of soaking at the end of the firing. Soaking means to hold the kiln at that final temperature, thus allowing all the glaze to

melt without the risk of overfiring. To soak, cover up the flue ever so slightly and cut back on the gas and air just a bit. If you cover up the flue too much, you will be back in a reduction mode. For our purposes, this would give us the same beneficial maturing effect to the glazes as soaking, but you may not want the reduction effects. Cutting back on the fuel too much will result in a cooling effect, which benefits nothing.

Is there an optimum firing length? This question comes up periodically. As far as its effect on the quality of the glazes, the firing time in raku is not as important as it is for a high-fire cycle. The length of firing should be governed by common sense regarding the safe, successful firing of your ware.

Unloading and the Postfiring Technique

Having achieved glaze meltage, the next phase is the removal of the ware from the kiln and postfiring reduction. The usual method for removing ware is by using tongs. Tongs are relatively easy to learn how to use and they keep you a safe distance from your glowing ware. Tongs may or may not leave a mark on your pot at the point of contact. In traditional raku firing, the tongs are cooled in water before reaching into the kiln. The cool tongs immediately harden the glaze and prevent an impression from being formed. In your firing, the first pots may show tong marks, but as the ware still in the kiln cools, tong marks are less likely. At any rate, tong marks should not be viewed as a defect but rather as an integral effect of the raku technique.

Grabbing your pots with tongs may seem straightforward, and for the most

6–13
Grabbing your ware with tongs is a safe and relatively easy skill to master.

that have proved to be versatile. These are lightweight and easily hammered into more customized shapes if you so desire. The beautiful pair of tongs at the top of Figure 6–14 were hand-forged in England and are sold by Roger and Lindsey Watts of Kent Pottery Tools. They are a pleasure to use. Fireplace supply shops are a good source for tongs, but beware of cheap, low-grade construction designed more for display than use. Tongs should be sturdily made of strong material such as iron or aluminum with substantial pins or bolts at the joint. I have never had a set of tongs fall apart during use, but I can imagine the disappointment I would feel if they did. I have also had some tongs made for me by a class at a local industrial school. The teacher was more than amiable in having a new and interesting project to assign his students. Be resourceful!

Grasping pots firmly but carefully is one of the more difficult skills to master. It will take some practice to be sensitive to your own strength when squeezing your ware with the tongs. Avoid touching thin rims and necks, and allow the weight of the piece to hang freely, thereby eliminat-

part it is. But first a few words about tongs. Tongs are available in different shapes and sizes and you will want ones that are appropriate for your pots. The most readily available tongs are manufactured by Kemper and come in two shapes

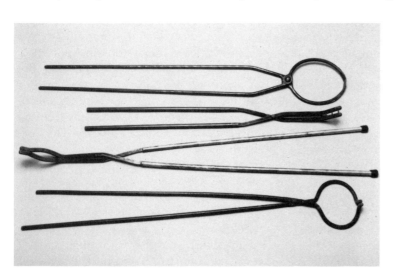

6–14
The tongs at the top are hand-forged from Kent Pottery Supply. The two in the middle are Kemper tongs. The bottom pair was made by the author.

ing unnecessary stress on the clay. It is generally easier to grab your pots with one jaw on the inside and one on the outside (see Fig. 6–13) than by wrapping the jaws of the tongs around the outside. Depending on the shape of the pot and the extent of the glazed surface, the pot may slip out of your grasp. Narrow-necked forms, unless the neck is so thin in relation to the weight of the pot, can usually be held under the rim by the tongs. Keep the piece perfectly upright and you won't place unnecessary stress on the neck.

Another method is one developed by Steven Kemenyffy for lifting his and his

6–15

Lifting a bottle from the kiln by carefully holding it under the rim.

wife Susan's large pieces. Incorporated into the design of the piece is a hole running through it. Steven inserts a steel rod through the hole and lifts the entire piece. Alternatively, some pieces are not lifted at all but are tilted with an iron rod or tongs onto a plywood platform (soaked with water to prevent burning) and then carried to the reduction pit and slipped in. Steven and Susan fire in a front-loading kiln, which gives them the easy access to their pieces necessary for this technique to work.

Yet another method of removing your pots is by lifting them with your gloved hands without using tongs. While you might think that not having to master the use of those long tongs will make life easier, gloves have disadvantages:

- The thickness of the gloves reduce dexterity.
- The crowded firing chamber makes grabbing pieces without disturbing others tricky.
- Gloves will leave marks on glazed surfaces.
- Gloves that will allow dexterity will not offer enough protection from the heat.

Use your hands, without tongs, only when you have absolutely no other way to proceed or for removing large pieces that physically cannot be lifted with tongs. When lifting without tongs:

- Wear *long* gloves and *complete* body protection.
- Use a second pair of gloves as "pot holders" to ensure protection from the hot ware.
- Wear a face mask, not just goggles.
- Go through a dry run beforehand to make sure you can physically lift the

6–16

A method of lifting a large piece developed by Steven and Susan Kemenyffy.

piece and be able to place it in your reduction container.

Contact with your work like this can be scary and intimidating, and that's reason enough to recommend a practice run. You will gain confidence and dispel some of your fears. However, there is nothing like doing the real thing for the first time! It is possible to lift out large or heavy pieces in a team of two, with each grabbing opposite sides of the piece. This requires exacting teamwork and communication lest you end up with two or more pieces for the price of one!

Objects that are too small to be lifted with tongs also present removal problems. The only effective way of removing beads

or other small objects (and avoiding your second raku-induced nervous breakdown at the same time) is to load them onto a small kiln shelf or into a suitable clay container that *can* be grabbed with the tongs. When the firing is ready, you can remove the container or shelf and dump the individual pieces into your reduction container. Or you can use a bead tree; in this case, simply put the entire tree in the reduction container.

Unloading the kiln begins with turning off the gas at the burner or switching off the elements in an electric kiln. Although it is common practice to simply turn down the burner to a flicker, I see no reason to leave the burner on. It doesn't keep the chamber hot for the next load and it is no

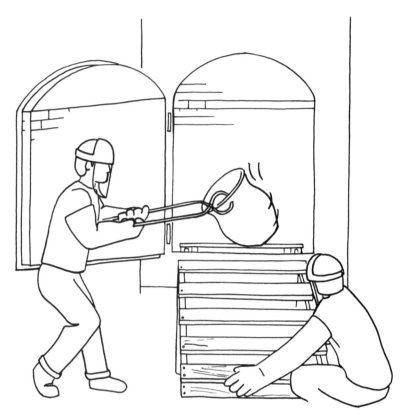

big deal to relight the burner for the next firing. Besides, you will encounter enough of a hot blast in your face without a lit burner adding to it.

For a wood-fired kiln, you will simply cease stoking. Expect flames from wood that is still burning in the chamber. Open the kiln or, in the case of a top-loader, remove the lid. Be sure you have prepared a safe, fire-resistant spot for the lid to rest on. For example, don't rest the lid on the grass or against a fence or tree. Better to place it on a brick or concrete block. For a top-loading electric kiln, *do not remove the lid from the kiln*. Use the hinge and lift the handle with tongs. Practice this beforehand with a cold kiln, being careful not

to get the tongs caught between the handle and the top course of bricks or electrical boxes when you close the kiln.

Position yourself comfortably to avoid back stress by not having to reach too far for either the pots or for placement in the reduction containers. For a top-loader, simply stand on a prepared platform of concrete blocks.

Removing your work from the kiln and the ensuing postfiring reduction is the heart of Western-style raku. To increase your chances of success, preparation and speed are essential. As before, I cannot stress the importance of preparation enough.

Place a layer of reduction material—

6–18
The author removing a piece from the firing with gloves only.

6–19
Tongs should be used to lift the lid of an electric kiln. The radiant heat is too severe for only gloved hands.

any carbon-based material—in each container. Sawdust is most popular, with leaves, hay, and paper following closely. Lumberyards, sawmills, and cabinet and furniture manufacturers are but a few of the many free sources for sawdust and other wood scraps. Have the containers and materials in place and the order of events clear in your mind.

For straightforward, no-frills postfiring reduction, shut off the gas, open the kiln, lift out your pieces, and place them in your containers as fast as you can. Just as you were careful in lifting your pots with the tongs, you must be careful when you

let them down in the containers. Try to place the ware gently, carefully letting go with the tongs so you don't nick the rim as you pull the tongs away. Once the ware is inside the container, add more reduction material and cover the container within 15 seconds to ensure efficient smoking for glaze and clay-body development. *You must cover the container tightly or a sudden burst of flames could blow the cover off the container.* Likewise, if for some reason, you uncover a container that is smoking a pot, either to place another piece in the container or to add additional reduction material, stand back with your face protected. The mixture of air with the heat in the container will cause a sudden flare-up that can be powerful as well as scary.

The basic reduction technique, if every step is done correctly (glaze application, firing to maturity, etc.), will result in crackled glazes, matt black clay, and metallic

6–20
Reduction containers in place for a firing.

lusters. Paramount to achieving these effects is *speed.*

If you have a helper assisting with the reduction phase, leather work gloves are adequate for handling the container covers and reduction materials. Of course Kevlar gloves, necessary for all the other raku work, are perfectly suitable as well. Addi-

tional reduction material should be dropped into the containers from close range. Don't *throw* the reduction material into the container; lightweight materials such as sawdust will simply blow around and end up all over the place. Hot air coming from the container can also blow away the material, creating a fire hazard.

6–21
Geoff Pagen removing one of his pieces from the kiln. Because Geoff's pieces are flat, he has prepared a reduction container of concrete blocks. Courtesy Geoff Pagen.

6–22

Geoff reduces in straw and covers the container with a lid fashioned of sheet metal with a wooden handle. Note the use of gloves, Kevlar sleeves, and eye protection. Courtesy Geoff Pagen.

Of course, you may already have enough reduction material in the container and may not need to add more after you place your piece inside. Don't be afraid of the flames coming from the container. As long as you are protected with gloves and the appropriate clothing, the flames won't hurt you. The initial burst of smoke during the postfiring reduction phase will last only about 30 seconds to a minute and may be no more noticeable than the smoke from a barbecue.

Let me stress that *it is not how much reduction material you use, but how fast you can get the material in the container and tightly covered.* The more airtight the seal, the better the reduction and the less smoke you will create. If you are doing raku in your yard and would rather not attract too much attention, this can be critical.

The best seal for a reduction container can be achieved by digging a shallow pit just slightly wider than the diameter of the rim of your container. Place your pot in the depression, apply your reduction material, and cover it with the inverted container. (See Fig. 6–23) Shovel some dirt or sand around the edge of the container to seal in the smoke and prevent oxygen from entering the chamber.

While we are on the subject of not attracting too much attention, let me stress again the importance of planning ahead and trying to anticipate any problems. Early in my raku experience, I was preparing to fire in a relatively populated area and I was concerned about attracting attention to this scary looking process. My firing area was behind a row of small retail shops. I located the kiln far enough from the building and any other flammable sources to be safe and had planned out all other aspects of the firing. All went fine, including the postfiring reduction, with very little smoke. It was over and I was fi-

6–23

Place your pot in the depression, apply your reduction material, and cover it with the inverted container.

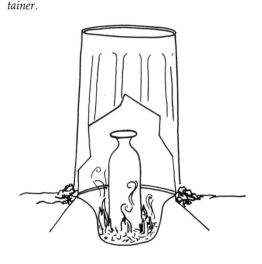

nally calm. A few minutes later I heard the sound of fire engines roaring down the block. Needless to say, I jumped. It turned out that one of the shops, an ice cream parlor no less, had filled with just enough smoky odor to alarm them. I hadn't anticipated their ventilation system, located on the roof of the building, sucking in the smoke, however little it was, from my firing. Of course by the time the fire trucks arrived, the smoking had stopped and everything behind the building seemed normal. Soon thereafter we moved our raku kilns to a friend's house in the country.

If you are doing large or unwieldy work that you simply cannot lift out of the kiln either with tongs or your hands, try reducing the piece in place. If you are us-

ing a fiber kiln where the entire chamber lifts off to expose the pots, place your reduction materials in a container and invert it over the pot or pots as they are stacked in place. Seal up the burner port and any other places where air can enter the chamber. Be sure that your container will fit over the pots, both in width and height. This is an effective postfiring reduction method providing you can get a good seal between the rim of the container and the base of the chamber. A strip of fiber used as a gasket will usually solve the problem.

If you are firing a top- or front-loading brick kiln, shut off the burner, close up the peep holes and burner port, and drop or shovel your reduction materials into the kiln. (Figs. 6–24, 6–25) Immediately cover the flue and make the chamber as airtight

6–24
Douglas Johnson shoveling sawdust into the kiln for the postfiring reduction phase. Courtesy Douglas Johnson.

6–25
Pots and wet sawdust coming out of kiln.

I never use water to force-cool my work, although it is not completely unsafe to use water for small or moderate-sized work. Why risk cracking, though, by fast cooling? Be patient. If you do use the speed-cool method, here are some tips. Try to dunk your pot as quickly as possible to avoid cooling one side while the other is hot, setting up a shocking situation! When water-cooling a small-necked form, you must not submerge the opening all at once, the pressure buildup can shatter the piece. Allow the water to enter the piece carefully and slowly until it fills up. Because of the shape, if it fills too quickly, the water will boil and spit out the top like a geyser. This can be scary as well as dangerous. As the piece is filling, pour water on the outside to cool it as evenly as possible. The buoyancy of a hollow form like that will make it difficult to submerge slowly. Be careful not to break the neck. A cautionary note about water cooling that may or may not be obvious: Hot pots quickly heat up the water buckets they are placed in, so be careful when reaching in to retrieve your ware.

Reloading the Kiln and Subsequent Firings

To fire multiple loads of raku successfully, the next batch of pots *must have been preheating* during the previous firing. Again, remember that most breakage occurs when going from cold to hot, so be patient here. The more porous and shock-resistant your clay body, the more success you will have in firing multiple loads. Yes, I too have seen cold pots put in a preheated kiln with no breakage. Treat this event as a miracle gift from the kiln god, lest she think you greedy. Make it a habit to preheat your ware. Glaze is also subject to

as possible. I have gotten mixed results when using this technique, mostly because it is difficult in a brick kiln to create a chamber that is airtight enough for effective smoking.

In workshop situations, I keep the work in the containers until the next batch of pots is ready to come out, anywhere from 15 minutes to an hour. This is sufficient for most work. For my own work, I keep the pots covered for a good two hours, or until the smoking has completely stopped. This is mostly to ensure slow cooling, important for work 24″ tall and larger.

Plate 12
*Dick Lehman. Untitled. 7"h. Copper-stained raku
(see recipe) with leaf imaging. Courtesy the artist.*

Plate 13
*Author. Vase. 22"h. 1989. Combed surface.
Brushed and sponged oxides under a clear glaze.
Lightly fumed with silver nitrate. Photo: Robert Ar-
ruda.*

Plate 14
Robert Bede Clark. Ewer. 19"h × 11½"w. 1990.
Saggar-fired earthenware. Courtesy the artist.

Plate 15
Jan Jacque. Sea Ray Vessel. 17"h × 23"w × 7"d. Hand-built. The ware is air-brushed with colored slips and then bisque fired. Smoke firing in sawdust, leaves, and grasses results in beautiful, subtle surfaces. Courtesy the artist.

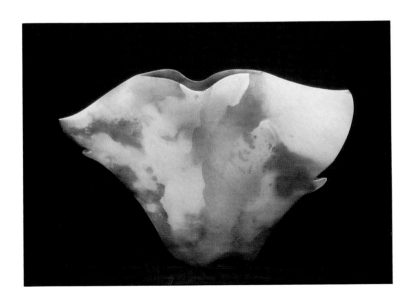

Plate 16
Chuck Hindes. Shield. 30"h × 24"w × 7"d. Cone 04, fired in a temporary brick saggar topped with kiln shelves. Courtesy the artist.

Plate 17

Paul Soldner. Wheel thrown and altered form. 29½"h × 41"w × 8"d. Impressed surface texture from paddling and rolling the form on canvas and burlap. A variety of slips, stains, and oxides were applied prior to the low-temperature salt firing. Courtesy the artist.

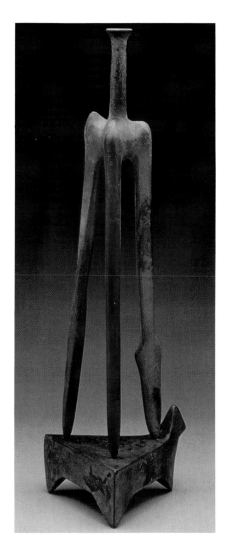

Plate 18

Rick Hirsch. Vessel and Stand #21. Coper-Metti Series. 25"h × 7½"w. 1987. Colored terra sigilattas. Photo: Dean Powell.

Plate 19

Bryan McGrath. Bowl. 13"h × 13"d. 1990. Thrown and altered. The piece was sprayed with a solution of lithium, borax, and Jordan Clay before raku firing. Courtesy the artist.

Plate 20

Jim Romberg. Temple Jar. 24"h × 12"w. 1989. Glazes, slips, and oxides were applied by brushing, spraying, and pouring. Careful manipulation of the smoking phase results in a varied surface. Courtesy the artist.

Plate 21

Wayne Higby. Blue Water Noon. 1990. 13"h × 19½"w × 15"d. Thrown and altered. Reduction in damp straw leaves distinct impressions in the glaze and results in the copper glaze turning blue and not metallic. Photo: Steve Myers.

Plate 22

Gail Yurasek. Triptych. 24" × 35". 1989. Torn, sandwiched slabs are draped over a Styrofoam form and the edges are pressed down with a board. Commercial glazes and underglazes are used sparingly for color. A silver nitrate glaze is sprayed over a basic white glaze, resulting in blushes of pink. Courtesy the artist.

Plate 23
John Hodge. Untitled. *12"h.
1990. Commercial glazes are
brushed over wax resist and
pencil-drawn lines. Fumed
with ferric chloride and reduced in hay and sawdust.
Courtesy the artist.*

heat shock of a sort, so again be sure the glaze is dry before you load the piece into the kiln.

Common practice is to place the pots on the top of the kiln, heating them with the radiant heat from the kiln. Rotate the pots frequently, and don't allow them to block the flue. Aside from pots interfering with the draft, pieces placed that close to the flue can actually get too hot on one side and crack. You may also notice a piece turning black as it sits atop the kiln. This is simply carbon, which will fire off once you place the ware in the kiln. If, however, your kiln is particularly tight, with little heat radiating from the top, then preheating in this manner will not be effective.

Proceed with extreme caution when loading your ware into the kiln. Successfully preheated pots are too hot to touch without gloves! When the current batch is ready to be unloaded, if you are using a top-loader, make sure you have a safe place where you can set the preheated pots. Unload, do your postfiring, and you're ready to reload the kiln.

Using either tongs or your gloved hands, place the pots in the kiln. When using a top-loader, I place the pots around the rim of the kiln to continue preheating before I place them in the kiln (Fig. 6–27). Some say I am overly cautious, and perhaps I am. Experiment to see what works best for you. For larger work, or in situations when you are doubtful as to how well the pots have preheated, use a cold hardbrick or insert a cold kiln shelf on top of the existing kiln shelf as a base for the next piece. Heat shock on the foot of the pot and on the pot as a whole will be minimized. This is a very effective means of assuring success in firing multiple loads. Cover or close the kiln, close the damper and insert all the peep-hole plugs, and leave the burner off for a minute or two to allow the pieces to continue to preheat.

6–26

Preheating ware on top of the kiln.

6–27

Top loaders can be used to preheat pots before placing them in the kiln.

If at this point you still see an orange glow at the burner port (unlikely), you will be able to turn on the gas and have the existing heat ignite the burners. If the port looks dark, then use newspaper and a match or spaker to light the burner. Be sure to uncover the flue first. Start slow, using similar guidelines in increasing the temperature as before, realizing that you *can go faster* than when starting with a cold kiln. If anything should break in the early stages of heating, open the kiln and remove the broken shards, especially those that might have landed inside or on an unharmed work.

Electric kilns, because of their slow cooling and lack of instantaneous temperature control, are as a rule not suitable for firing multiple loads. In addition, the *prolonged* exposure (versus quick opening and closing) of the hot face and elements to the cool air that would be necessary in order to reload the kiln would surely shorten the life of the kiln. I suppose that if you had a clay body that was particularly resistant to heat shock and you didn't care about the potential negative effect on the kiln, it could be done, but multiple loads really should be assigned to fuel-burning kilns.

6–28

Kendell Coniff. Raku Vessel. Thrown and hand-built. 10" × 7". The body is covered with a copper-saturated glaze resulting in a varied surface. Courtesy the artist. Photo: Rick Lucas.

Additional Postfiring and Decorative Techniques

Once you become familiar and confident with the basic raku technique, I hope you will experiment with other processes, using your imagination as a guide, as well as trying things you may have heard or read about. You may find yourself hesitant to try a technique you come across in an article or book, feeling you don't have enough information to get you going. Go ahead anyway, combining the knowledge you have with the new information. You'll often be pleasantly surprised at the results.

Typical postfiring reduction technique as I have just described has as its main objective matt black unglazed surfaces, metallic luster effects, and heavily crazed areas. I say "typical" not to malign those effects, for there is much about them to keep one busy technically and creatively for some time, but rather to indicate that these are the effects most potters are familiar with and most anxious to achieve in their initial encounter with raku. Once you become acquainted with these techniques, you can move on to more complicated ones.

Additional postfiring techniques revolve around the development of further kinds of glaze and surface effects, more sophisticated imagery, and the use of various types of reduction materials in an effort to control and shape more carefully the final results. Success in all these areas begins with the *correct* application of your glaze, slip, or oxide (if desired) and sufficient maturity in the kiln. Then you can rely primarily on a decisive reduction technique.

Glazes that are applied too thin will look matt and dry and will not display the richness in color or crackle effects that are so desirable to the raku potter. Remember that beauty is in the eye of the beholder, and who is to say what is a defect and what isn't? Many beautiful and distinctive effects have been obtained by intentionally thinning out a glaze or underfiring it.

Crazing, or crackling, is another sought-after effect. All raku glazes craze. Dark ones tend to not show off the crackle because of the dark color. Crazing, or crackling, can be accentuated by the direct contact of the reduction material and the surface of the piece. Crazing also is often dependent on a thick layer of glaze that is well fired to maturity.

I mentioned earlier the use of various types of materials for your reduction phase. As I said, any carbon-based material can be used. The list includes, but is certainly not limited to, sawdust (fine or coarse) and its various forms (chips, shavings), straw, hay, leaves, pine needles, fruit and vegetable peelings and skins, rags, and paper products. You can also experiment with different kinds of wood. I have come across potters who swear by cherry wood, oak, or poplar, or another species. I think it is not the *kind* of wood as much as the *form* of the wood—chips, fine sawdust, shavings—that makes the difference. Nevertheless, given the number of potters who disagree with me, different kinds of wood are certainly worth trying.

While experimenting with a variety of reduction materials may seem logical, the condition of the material also may affect the reduction results. Three major factors here are particle size (as in the case of sawdust), density (as in different thicknesses of cloth), and dryness. Dry material ignites immediately, burns hot, and results in the strongest reduction effects. To manipulate these effects, open the reduction container for brief periods, then close it to allow oxidation and cooling to take place. Another approach is to use damp or wet reduction materials. Wayne Higby uses damp straw to help cool the piece while reduction is taking place (see color Plate 21). This process gives his surfaces contact with the material and results in different textures; the amount of smoking results in color effects but prevents the reoxidation effects that would result in removing the ware from the straw.

Direct contact with your reduction material will leave traces of some sort on your pieces. On a glazed surface, the material will leave physical impressions in the glaze if the glaze hasn't hardened sufficiently before the piece came in contact with the material. On unglazed surfaces, contact with the material may leave areas of intense black, mottled effects, or other telltale signs of contact. Reduction materials such as pine needles or wood with a heavy resin content may leave surfaces with a slight sheen, almost as if you had rubbed the piece with oil. Experiment, and if you want to eliminate these effects, either prepare an area free of reduction material to accommodate your piece or elevate the piece on a brick within the reduction material. In both cases you will avoid contact between the molten glaze and the reducing agent. You may have to sprinkle in some fine sawdust or have a sheet of paper touch the piece in order to ignite the reduction material.

Sometimes you may want to cool your piece, thus hardening the glaze, before you apply our reduction material. The harder the glaze, the less smoking will affect it. Experiment by allowing your piece to cool for a certain amount of time before placing it in the reduction container. This cooling may take place in the kiln, after shutting off the gas, or outside the kiln. The Kemenyffys cool their work for ten

minutes in the kiln with the gas shut off and the door closed, and then for another minute with the door open before moving it to the reduction pit. There they are careful to use only sheets of cardboard as reduction agents in order to avoid the kind of intense local areas of reduction that can come from contact with fine materials like sawdust or straw. It is the combination of the harder glaze and their reduction style that gives them their desired results. Since their work is large, their pieces retain more heat and cool more slowly than a smaller piece would. A much shorter cooling time would be appropriate for smaller pieces. For an average thrown pot 10″ tall, try cooling it in the air for 15–30 seconds before placing it in the reduction container.

6–29
Susan and Steven Kemenyffy. The Dreyfus Study. 1987. Raku mural. Slab-built, incised and carved. About 6½′ × 6½′. Courtesy the artists.

An oil-impregnated rag or a bed of oil-soaked material also offers interesting reduction effects. The oil causes intense local reduction that often results in strong metallic effects and a fine network of small crazing and crackles. I have also had good results using oil on a copper matt surface. Avoid using fresh, clean motor oil. It is too rich and almost always leaves an oily residue on the ware that is difficult to wash off. Used motor oil works well and is abundant and free! Inquire at your local service station. Exercise caution when using oil. It ignites immediately and creates a lot of smoke.

Water is an effective postfiring medium. Remove your piece from the kiln and place it on a brick or concrete block. Spray water on a section of your pot to stop the reduction process while applying sawdust or an oil-soaked rag to another section. Other postfiring techniques include the application of additional reduction material after the piece has been in the container smoking. Lift off the lid carefully and expect a sudden burst of flame. Apply additional material and re-cover. This will often result in a darker unglazed surface.

If you are interested in intense luster and black effects achieved through concentrated smoking, you will need to learn more about the properties and characteristics of smoke and carbon and how to regulate them. Your ware, depending on its surface treatment of slip, glaze, underglaze, oxide, or Mason Stain, reacts differently to the smoking of postfiring reduction. Each has its own degree of "resist" to the carbon, which affects its absorption of it. An example is the "halo" effect developed by Paul Soldner and subsequently adapted by many potters using their own versions of the technique.

Kerry Gonzalez uses commercial underglazes to which he adds borax in small amounts as flux. The mixture is applied with a slip trailing bottle and tends to melt slightly more toward the edges of his designs. In a soft, even-smoking atmosphere created by using newspapers as the reduction material, the carbon is resisted by the fluxed edges, resulting in the halo. A bed of opened, uncrumpled newspaper cradles the pot. Gerstley borate may be better than borax because of borax's granular nature and solubility. Kerry adds just a few grams per 3-ounce bottle of underglaze. This technique is laden with nuance, so you must experiment with it to achieve the proper maturing temperature and degree of reduction. A logical way to proceed in determining the correct firing temperature would be to include the piece in a load of your regularly glazed pots. Use a pyrometer to monitor the temperature. Since the amount of melting is so small

6–30

Laying an oil-soaked rag over a piece affords a heavy reduction that often yields a spectrum of colors.

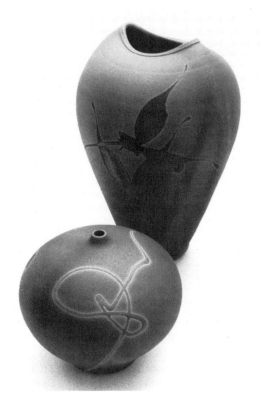

6–31
*Kerry Gonzalez. (Left) Weed Bottle. 1990.
Thrown. 6" h. (Right) Ovoid Vase. 1990. Thrown
and altered. 12" h. Both pieces display the artist's
version of the halo effect. Courtesy the artist.*

and difficult to observe, remove the piece
when the rest of the load is mature and
assess the results. If you have too much
gloss, lower the temperature the equivalent of one cone. If you need more melting, raise the temperature one cone.

Jim Romberg manipulates the smoking
phase to achieve certain effects. He deco-
rates his pots with a variety of glazes,
slips, and oxide mixtures of copper, cobalt, and iron. He uses a variety of application techniques as well, including pouring, brushing, and spraying with an

atomizer. The key for Jim, though, is carefully controlling the reduction through the
use of newspaper and a series of reoxidation steps: opening the container, placing
more newspaper on certain areas of the
piece, and moderate resmoking by partially closing the container. His work dis-
plays dark areas where the reduction was
heavy, as well as gray to white areas that
are the result of little smoking.

Jerry Caplan has developed an interesting reduction technique. He applies a
slip formulated for application to a wet
piece to the surface of a bisque-fired bowl
or platter form. While the slip is wet, he

6–32
*Jim Romberg lifts off the lid of a container to reoxi-
dize a piece. Courtesy Jim Romberg.*

6–33
*Jim Romberg. En-
trées et Sorties.
Raku-fired wall relief.
5' h × 7' w. In-
stalled at Vector Elec-
tronics, Sylmar, Cali-
fornia, 1987.
Courtesy the artist.
See color Plate 21.*

carves a pattern through the slip with a needle or other fine-pointed tool. Because it is not formulated for application to bisque ware, the slip naturally curls away from the surface into "islands" as it dries. Carefully, so as to not disturb the patterns, he places the ware in the kiln and fires to maturity, approximately 1800 degrees F. Equally carefully, he removes the ware from the kiln and places it face up on a flat surface covered with sheets of folded newspaper. He places more folded newspaper over the top of the piece and covers the work with a trash-can lid or inverted container. The reduction process must be quick and the container must have a tight seal. Jerry ensures a virtually airtight seal by using a ring of sand 1–2" deep as a gasket upon which the container sits. The now-fired slip that remains on the piece acts as a resist to the smoking of postfiring reduction. Cooling takes about 10 minutes. The ware is taken from the container and the slip resist is emptied off as it is not fused to the ware. Jerry washes the work to remove any residue and slip

that may have adhered to the surface. This resist-type technique imparts a soft, quiet character to the piece (Fig. 6–34). The white clay gives way gradually to grays and blacks, depending on the character of the crawled clay-slip shapes. Jerry has since introduced color to his work by adding commercial underglazes. The underglazes are applied to the greenware and develop where they are protected from smoking by the cover of slip.

The copper matt effect itself can be difficult and frustrating to achieve. It is in fact as much a postfiring technique as a glazing or decorating technique. Begin by applying a *thin layer* of copper matt stain for the most consistent results; the layer will seem almost too thin. The most effective means of application is spraying. Use an airbrush with compressor, atomizer, or a simple spray bottle. At The Wesleyan Potters in Connecticut, I was introduced to a garden sprayer that works by pumping up its pressure. It was very effective.

Place some reduction material in your container and place your piece on a brick.

6–34
Jerry Caplan. Bowl. 1989. Reduction stenciling.
14" d. Courtesy the artist.

cess quite accidentally when a piece of his straight out of the kiln rolled down an embankment into some wet grass. He retrieved the pot, put it in the reduction container, and upon examining it afterward noticed a remarkable photo-like image of the grass on the pot. (Fig. 6–35 and color Plate 13) Dick sprays a copper matt stain on the ware in a very thin layer. He has used a mouth atomizer, an atomizer connected to a compressor, and a conventional air brush and compressor, all with excellent results.

If applied too thick, the copper matt will flux and the subtlety or even the en-

6–35
Dick Lehman. Vase. 1987. Copper-stained raku
with leaf imaging. 11" h. Courtesy Dick Lehman.

The brick will isolate the piece from prolonged, direct contact with the material. Place some reduction material over the piece and close the container quickly. My former assistant, Mark DelloRusso, achieves consistent results using this technique with dry leaves as his reduction material. (See color Plate 10)

A variation of the copper matt effect is to rub a thin iron oxide wash or dry ion oxide into the surface of the piece. The iron will act as a resist to the carbon, resulting in an earthy surface reminiscent of reduction-fired stoneware clay or the familiar yellow matt effect. To achieve this result, partially reoxidize the piece after a brief 2–3 minute period of smoking, by uncovering the container and adding more reduction material.

A technique combining the copper matt effect and direct contact with reduction materials is shared by Indiana potter Dick Lehman. Dick came across this pro-

tire effect will be lost. Some experimentation will be necessary to arrive at the correct thickness, but if it looks too thin, it is probably correct! Firing proceeds at a normal raku pace. Dick fires 20-minute cycles in a fiber-lined garbage can with natural gas. In a departure from the usual, he uses a small cone 011 to guide his firings. Actually, using a cone when firing a load of all copper matt pots is a good idea since you have no melted glaze to judge maturity. Upon cone 011 flat, Dick removes the pots from the kiln and places them out in the open on a bed of prepared sawdust covered with fresh-picked leaves and grasses. After 30–45 seconds, color begins to develop on the side of the ware where the flames lick up. At this point the piece is covered (in place) and allowed to reduce completely. As a variation, uncover the piece after 5 minutes or so of reduction for 3–4 seconds of oxidation. Doing this will enhance color development. Remember that when uncovering a reducing container the possibility of a sudden flame-up is always present.

Lehman Copper Matt Stain

Barium carbonate	4.17
Borax	4.17
Copper carbonate	62.5
Lithium carbonate	12.5
Ferro frit 3134	16.66

This recipe (including the borax) is put through an 80-mesh screen.

Lehman Raku/Flameware Body cone 011–9
(bisque to cone 08)

Spodumene	30
Custer feldspar	10
[potash feldspar]	
Foundry Hill Creme Clay	30
OM 4 ball clay	20

Pyrophyllite	10
[hydrous aluminum silicate]	
Add: Bentonite	2
Macaloid	1

Note: Foundry Hill Creme Clay is an air-floated, fine-mesh fireclay with little if any limestone contaminants. You may substitute any quality fireclay with similar characteristics.

Fuming, or the application of metallic salts to the surface of your ware, is yet another technique whose roots are not in raku at all but has been adapted to the American raku process. Related to salt firing or vapor glazing, fuming can add lustrous gold, silver, and mother-of-pearl effects to glazed surfaces. Metallic salts, as noted in the section on glazes, can be used as a wash or as components of glazes. Their use here offers you an alternate method of application, which can result in different, though not necessarily better, effects.

The most common method of fuming is upon maturity. Remove the ware from the kiln and place it on a brick pad. Spray a solution of silver nitrate, stannous chloride, or other soluble salts onto the piece. As you do this, you can combine localized postfiring reduction techniques as well as water-cooling techniques to control the final outcome. In this case, try using water as a "fix" on the fumed area to lessen the chance of the fumed effect being a fleeting one. As the color develops, cool the area with a water spray or simply dunk the entire pot in water.

Fuming can also be carried out by introducing the salts into the kiln during the last stages of the firing, as in salt firing. Whatever method of fuming you try, protect yourself from fumes by working only outdoors while standing upwind. Other salts used in fuming include cobalt nitrate,

6–36
Fuming a piece with a spray of silver nitrate. Mask and gloves are worn to protect from fumes and the corrosive nature of the silver nitrate.

6–37
Author. Vase. 1987. Thrown with combed design. 20" h. Thin applications of a white glaze on the top portion and a copper glaze on the rest. The piece was fumed with silver nitrate and then reduced in sawdust, yielding a gentle iridescence. See color Plate 13. Photo: Robert Arruda.

cupric chloride, chromium nitrate, silver chloride, and zinc oxide. I repeat my cautionary note of before: metallic salts are corrosive, and silver nitrate will stain your skin and clothes. Wear rubber gloves. To prepare a salt spray for fuming, use the same guidelines as presented in the section on glazing.

Falling somewhere between fuming and vapor glazing and saggar firing, is the technique of placing salt, powdered oxides, and soluble salts in your reduction containers along with more conventional reducing materials, such as sawdust or straw. Upon ignition from the heat of your ware, these materials will volatilize to effect changes in your glazes and surfaces.

Possible variations on postfiring reduction methods are many and are limited only by your vision and ability to identify materials and conditions that may affect your ware in some way. Certainly the more experience you gain with documented techniques, the more knowledge you will have to apply to your own problem solving. As in any form of experimentation, limit the variables and stick to one change in technique at a time. Otherwise, an effect, whether or not desirable, may be impossible to track back to its cause.

Finishing Your Ware

Chapter 7

Your ware is fired, cooled, and beautiful. It's done! Not quite. The raku process, particularly the postfiring reduction phase, imparts a lustrous sheen to the glazed surface of the ware. Not to be confused with the luster effects of copper matt, this sheen is a layer of carbon and soot that may appear as a shiny, silver coating. You don't really need to be able to recognize it because it will become evident as you wash it off.

If having to wash your ware is news to you, I'm not surprised. Many times I have enlightened potters who have done raku before about washing the ware. Washing must be vigorous but also done with care because of raku's fragility. A stiff-bristled nail brush or a toothbrush for small pieces and crevices is the best tool to use. You can also use those "greenie" abrasive cleaning pads, but I have found them to be not as effective. Steel wool or Brillo pads can be used as well, but they are often too abrasive and can scratch the surface depending on the hardness of your glaze.

Along with a brush, an abrasive cleaner is an absolute necessity. I have done exhaustive tests to determine the most effective cleaner to use and the winner is . . . Ajax. I have tried various brand-name cleaners, but when it comes to cleaning raku, Ajax outcleans them all. Wet the piece and use liberal amounts of cleaner directly on the ware. You don't have to scrub unglazed areas unless you have used a coloring oxide or slip. As you wash off the sheen, the true colors of your work become exposed. This will be particularly noticeable on white and light-colored surfaces. As the piece dries, the cleaner's white residue will remain on the unglazed surfaces and you will find this difficult to remove. Rinse and scrub with water until it washes away.

7–2
Christine Shadic. Plate. *Thrown; combed pattern. 14" d.*

7–3
Judith E. Motzkin. Spirit Vessel with Woven Lid. *1990. Wheel-thrown and altered; terra sigillata. Sawdust pit fired. 10" × 10". Photo: Tom Lang.*

Scenario: A piece emerges from the reduction container in two pieces, or a piece of the rim is broken off, or something else has ruined an otherwise successful work. Suddenly the devious thought of gluing the piece back together enters your mind. Quickly, you seek out counseling for your affliction. Well, go ahead and glue the thing back together. Keep in mind that historically gold and silver were melted and used to fill cracks in pottery. If you do choose to glue, I have found that an adhesive called Durabond, manufactured by Duro, works well. Or try any epoxy adhesive. Apply the glue sparingly toward the inside edge of the crack so that it doesn't ooze onto the surface and mar your work.

To ink or not to ink? that is the question. An equally devious post-postfiring technique is to accentuate the crackle in your glazes by rubbing the surface with ink. In Asia tea was used for the same purpose on celadon ware.

Finally, what about waterproofing your ware? Because of the porosity of the clay body, crackle glazes, and extreme heat shock, the ware is rendered fragile and is not waterproof. Some potters have used urethane, tung oil, and a variety of other coatings in an attempt to seal the ware from the inside. Although I have never used it, I understand that tung oil is effective. Whatever coating you use, the piece should never hold food or drink. I treat my work as decorative and advise my customers to put a plastic or glass liner in the pot if they want to use it for flowers or plants.

Related Techniques

Chapter **8**

Partly due to confusion and partly to experimentation and advances in techniques, other pottery processes are linked to raku in different ways. Among these are pit firing, smoke and sawdust firing, saggar firing, and vapor glazing, including salt, soda, and fuming. Of these, pit and sawdust firing are most often confused with raku by the novice or student.

Pit Firing

Pit firing has its roots in primitive cultures and is in fact the first form of "kiln fired" ware before there were kilns per se. Perhaps when ancient woman (or man) noticed that mud around the fire hardened to a more permanent state, she fashioned objects and placed them in the fire—and the rest is history. In its more refined state, pit firing is a controlled process where pieces are fired in a shallow pit surrounded by wood or material such as dung, corn husks, or seaweed. The pit, with its methodically stacked ware and fuel, can easily reach bisque temperatures. (Fig. 8–1) Undoubtedly the particular fuel was dictated by culture and geography. The firing proceeds to maturity and cools naturally.

A variation on the open pit technique was developed by Maria Martinez and her family in the early part of this century. The open pit, fuel, and pots are covered with sheet metal scraps to form a kind of shell to increase temperatures. Upon maturity, the ware is smothered with finely ground dung and sawdust, creating a carbon-filled reducing atmosphere around the pots, not unlike postfiring reduction in raku. This stage of the firing is carefully monitored so that no smoke escapes and to prevent flame-ups. The ware is allowed to cool for some time before unloading. Pit

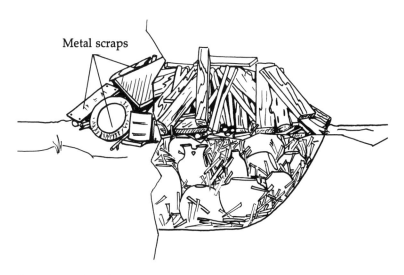

Metal scraps

8–1

Cutaway view of a pit firing showing metal scraps used as a shell.

firing in either form is essentially unrelated to the raku technique, except for perhaps the similarities in the reduction phase practiced by Maria.

Sawdust (Smoke) Firing

Sawdust, or smoke, firing is also often confused with raku firing. This modern innovation is no doubt based on pit or primitive firing. The concept behind sawdust firing is that the ware is completely surrounded by the fuel, including the insides of the pots. Firing is carried out in a simple structure designed merely to contain the work and the heat. The sawdust burns without flames, creating a hot, reducing atmosphere. A firing of this type may take anywhere from a few hours to a few days depending on the size of the kiln, the ware, wind conditions, and the type of sawdust used. It is important that after lighting the kiln and the sawdust has been ignited that the firing not be disturbed for the duration. When all smoldering and smoking has subsided, the firing is finished and the ware may be unloaded.

A sawdust kiln can be fashioned from a steel trash can, as shown in Figure 8–2. Prepare the can by drilling or poking holes approximately 1–2″ in diameter around the bottom and top circumference. Create more holes in a random fashion all around the can. The holes allow for adequate air infiltration to keep the fuel burning. Experimentation will be necessary to arrive at just the right amount of air flow. There should be no visible flames, only the smoldering of the sawdust. Plug any holes that seem unnecessary with refractory fiber.

Place in the can a 5″ layer of sawdust. On this, place your largest and heaviest ware. Surround the pots completely with sawdust and fill the ware as well. Cover with another layer of sawdust and continue for two or three courses of pots. Top off the container with some crumpled newspaper to act as kindling. Light the newspaper and cover the barrel as soon as the sawdust ignites. As the sawdust burns, the pots will settle onto each other, so be careful not to load the kiln with too much ware.

A brick kiln can be fashioned easily with common red brick, as shown in Figure 8–5. Build the first course loosely, leaving gaps between the brick for airflow.

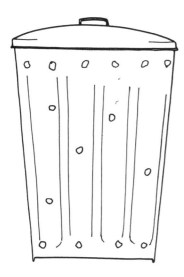

8–2
(A) A trash-can sawdust kiln. (B) Cutaway view showing stacking method.

Load your pots as you build up the kiln, leaving random gaps between bricks and a removable brick on each side of the kiln for more air. If additional air becomes unnecessary, simply plug up some of the spaces. Top off the kiln with a trash can cover, kiln shelves, or whatever you happen to have around. As a refinement, some potters place a shelf of chicken wire or hardware cloth between each course to protect the ware, while others create a chicken-wire container for each pot. Leon Nigrosh in his book *Low Fire* suggests punching an even row of holes at the same height on opposite sides of your trash can kiln and inserting iron bars to act as shelves.

Another form of smoke firing is more

8–3
Jan Jacque. Tear Oval. *Hand-built; airbrushed with colored slips; smoke-fired in a metal box with sawdust, leaves, and grasses. 8" h × 14" w × 5" d. See Color Plate 15. Courtesy the artist.*

8–4

Nancy Gilson. Traditional Pot. 1990. Wheel thrown, polished and incised; terra sigillata applied over the surface, sawdust-fired. 11" h × 8" w. Courtesy the artist. Photo: George Disario.

8–6

Harriet Brisson. Bowl. Combination sawdust-raku fired as described in the text. 4" × 4". Courtesy Harriet Brisson.

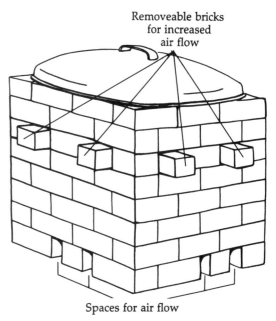

Removeable bricks
for increased
air flow

Spaces for air flow

8–5

A brick sawdust kiln. Note the air spaces in the bottom course of bricks and the removable bricks for increased airflow.

closely related to raku. In this process the unglazed pots are fired in a kiln, but upon reaching a predetermined temperature are removed and smoked in containers *à la* raku. Actually, this technique is so similar to American raku, except for glazing, that I probably should not distinguish between the two at all.

Harriet Brisson has developed an interesting technique combining sawdust firing and raku firing. She bisque fires pieces made from a red raku body, then fires them in sawdust in a metal trash can. Upon cooling, a clear glaze is applied and the piece is raku fired, including the typical postfiring reduction technique, in a charcoal-fired kiln. The heavily reducing atmosphere of the charcoal allows the subtle carbon shadows of the sawdust firing to remain intact under the glaze. A key aspect to Harriet's technique is the fact that her saggar has small holes in the walls to aid in the heat transfer from the coals as well as to allow flames to enter the saggar.

Vapor Firing

Vapor firing, whether you use rock salt, soda ash, baking soda, or some other form of salt, is a traditional form of firing developed in Germany in the twelfth to fifteenth centuries. As the salt vaporizes, the sodium combines with the silica (as the glass former) and alumina (for viscosity) contained in the clay and forms a glaze on the surface of the pot. Successful salt glazing depends on having a clay body that is mature at the time of salting. Thus salt firing can be carried out at any temperature, providing it is above the melting point of the salt (1472° F) and your clay is mature. Because salt firing does work at low temperatures, the technique became a natural attraction for those working in raku. It should be noted that salt glazing creates dangerous by-products, namely, hydrochloric acid and chlorine gas, that are avoided when using a substitute such as soda ash.

There are many ways to introduce salt into the firing. Traditionally, at the point of maturity of the clay, salt is introduced through ports above the burner ports. This can be done by pouring dry scoopfuls of salt into the port, by making a small "package" of salt with newspaper, or my favorite method—to use paper cups, twisting the tops closed to contain the salt. Some potters soak the salt packets in water before putting them in the kiln. I have found no difference in effects between wet or dry salt. Another convenient

8–7
Introducing salt into the firing through the flue.

method is to use a piece of angle iron as a ramp for pouring the salt into the port. (Fig. 8–7) Whichever means you use to introduce the salt, beware of exploding and spattering salt. The airborne particles can be dangerous.

The best way to determine whether salting is complete is to place some draw rings—that is, small rings of clay—in the kiln before you begin. Later, you can pull them from the kiln easily and after they have cooled, examine them for sufficient glaze development. Small glazed or otherwise decorated test pots can be even more helpful. For my 8-cubic foot kiln, I use 2 cups of salt, waiting ten minutes or so before introducing 2 more cups. From this point on I use the draw rings to determine completion of the firing.

When salting, the kiln should be in a reduction cycle to aid in color development and allow the vapor to circulate completely throughout the kiln. Other methods of introducing salt into the firing include soaking your pot in a saltwater solution before loading in the kiln, wrapping salt-soaked rags around you ware, and introducing salt into your postfiring reduction process.

Soluble salts used in fuming can also be introduced into the firing chamber. Depending on how much material you will introduce, use a long-handled spoon or the angle-iron method—a spoon for small amounts (silver nitrate, bismuth subnitrate) and the angle iron for larger amounts. You will need to experiment.

Should you use glazes, slips, or oxides on your ware when salt firing? Answer this question according to your own expectations and impulses. Experiment using the many different raku variations you are familiar with to arrive at your own way of working. When I said that successful salt glazing depends on a mature clay body, I meant that in the sense of achieving a true salt-glazed surface. That is not to say that colorful and otherwise interesting results are not obtained when salting is carried out on an immature clay body. In this case, the sodium vapor reacts with the

8–8
Paul Soldner. Wheel-thrown and altered form. 1986. Low-fire salt-fumed. 18" h × 18" w × 5½" d. Courtesy the artist.

slips, glazes, and other coloring materials on your ware, as well as reacting to a lesser degree with the clay body. Again, experimentation is necessary to satisfy your expectations.

Saggar Firing

Techniques of saggar firing have been adapted by raku potters. Involvement with saggar firing has at times brought people to raku as well as taken them away from it in their search for appropriate vehicles for their claywork. Saggar firing, as mentioned earlier, developed as a method of stacking ware in a kiln in order to isolate the ware from the potential negative results of contact with either the fuel itself or the flames. The potential for using saggars to create intense atmospheric conditions is another relatively recent development in the potter's creative arsenal.

8–9

Dane Venaas. Vessel. Wheel-thrown. 18" × 18". The piece was wrapped in fresh kelp and saggar-fired to 1000° C. Courtesy the artist. Photo: Mehosh Dzaidzio.

R. Bede Clark settled on saggar firing by experimenting with raku. His technique revolves around the building of temporary brick saggars in his kiln around his ware. Figures 8–10 through 8–13 illustrate Bede's stacking technique. The bisque-fired work is sometimes left free of any decoration, or Bede may rub or otherwise embellish it with washes of copper, soluble salts, brine, and slips. Loaded around the ware may be wood, sawdust, seaweed, and other organic material. Soluble salts, rock salt, and Epsom salt, as well as copper carbonate, iron oxide, and yellow ochre, are sprinkled on and around the ware. Fir-

8–10

Be careful not to impede heat flow or draft with the building or placement of your saggar in the kiln. Photo: Robert Bede Clark.

ing is carried out in about 5–6 hours to cone 010 in a downdraft gas-fired kiln. Here is Bede's clay body recipe:

White Salt/Saggar Body (Cone 010–04)

Talc	15
Wollastonite	5
A.P. Green fireclay	40
[Potclays fireclay 1275/3]	
Tennessee ball clay	25
[HVAR ball clay]	
Fine grog	7.5
Medium grog	7.5

8–11

Reducing materials such as sawdust, charcoal, and salt-soaked vermiculite, as well as salts and oxides, are packed around and sprinkled on the ware as the saggar is constructed. Photo: Robert Bede Clark.

Your particular firing situation (type of kiln, location, etc.) may or may not accommodate the use of a saggar. Instead, use the entire firing chamber as your saggar, loading in your ware along with organic material such as sawdust, wood, seaweed, fruit peelings, and salts. Expect heavily reducing conditions. Add more material as the firing progresses. Results obtainable through this type of firing are certainly varied and unpredictable, although they usually produce striking yet subtle effects (see color Plates 14 and 16). As in any experimentation, firing techniques and equipment that are more easily controlled, as in the use of an actual saggar as op-

8–12

The ware is surrounded with reduction materials up to their rims. Photo: Robert Bede Clark.

8–13

Once the saggar is capped with kiln shelves, other ware may be stacked on top. Photo: Robert Bede Clark.

8–14

Ben Parks. White Pyramid. 1990. 44" h × 30" w. The individual sections that make up this piece are hollow and are fired as though they were the saggars. Each piece is filled with salt, copper, sawdust, and charcoal briquettes. Fragments of old shelves used for salt firing are leaned against the exteriors and used for masking the surface and directing the fuming—a "saggar in reverse" technique. Courtesy the artist.

posed to a brick one, or using the entire chamber as a "saggar," will produce more predictable results.

When using a saggar, expect the temperature inside the saggar to be 1–2 cones below the temperature in the kiln chamber. In practical applications this means that if you are firing glazed ware in the saggar you must be able to view the work *while it is inside* to determine actual glaze melt. Check the glaze melt through a peep hole rather than lifting the lid of the saggar. By lifting the lid you may disturb the atmosphere that you have worked so hard

to create. Don't rely on the maturity of other pieces in the kiln that are perhaps stacked on top of the saggar to determine the finished state of the work. If you are firing unglazed ware decorated with oxides, salts, or slips, the firing temperature may not be as critical. When using saggar techniques, you may choose not to include the postfiring reduction phase as part of your cycle. Given the increased number of creative variables when using a saggar, you should absolutely experiment with the postfiring phase as opposed to including it automatically.

Are there other related techniques that may offer alternate paths for the raku potter? Can methods and procedures thought to be reserved for a singular pottery process be extended and incorporated into the raku technique? Imagination and bold experimentation are the keys to innovation and progress and may be the only things standing in your way.

Raku in the Classroom

Chapter 9

When I use the phrase "raku in the classroom," I am really referring to any situation where an attempt is made to teach the raku process through a hands-on participatory experience. Your interest may lie in the raku technique in and of itself, or, as Warren Gilbertson observed, you may be interested in using raku as a vehicle for introducing your students to pottery or crafts in general. Yours may be an elementary classroom, high school ceramics studio, adult education class, raku workshop, or any other teaching environment. You may be a skilled raku potter but lack teaching experience, or you may have limited raku expertise but have taught pottery for many years. Whatever your knowledge or expertise, there is a difference between *doing* and *teaching*. There are certainly wonderful teachers who are accomplished craftspeople with long, distinguished exhibition records. However, some of the best teachers have only limited exhibition and production histories, while those who we may expect to light our fires because of their work and stature in the field turn out to be inspirational duds.

Indeed integral to successful teaching of any kind is knowledge of the subject, but an understanding of how people learn is paramount. For example, as a teacher I have always had difficulty justifying the case for subjecting students to mundane mistakes that have been made before, all in the name of learning. That is not to say that students should be protected from making mistakes, because failure, or lack of immediate success, is certainly a strong impetus for learning. However, there are "mistakes" and there are mistakes. One of the joys of teaching is to be able to have your students avoid the obvious pitfalls for the sake of more relevant efforts in learning.

This is not a lesson on how to become a good pottery teacher! Teaching in and of itself is a difficult task to master, takes years of practice, and is best learned with a mentor on the job. I will merely point out some things that will make your effort at teaching raku more successful.

Raku in Schools

I am often asked whether raku firing is appropriate in a school situation. Is it too dangerous? Uncertainty stems from a doubt that the children can grasp the concepts, be involved physically, and be inspired. Questions of whether raku can be set up in *my* school situation and what the principal might think also come into play. While most of my comments here refer to elementary through junior high school students, much also applies to those of all ages.

It is no wonder that raku has become a popular pottery activity in schools. Kids as young as kindergarten through high school are being introduced to pottery through a hands-on experience with the raku technique. My feelings on using raku in this way are mixed. We as school teachers are always striving to elicit attentiveness and involvement from our students and ultimately motivate them. And it is clear that the excitement, speed, and unusual nature of the raku process enhances our efforts to do so. On the other hand, to oversimplify a long-standing craft technique of historical and cultural significance certainly does a disservice to it and to all of us who engage in it respectfully and in earnest. Simply stated, when raku takes on an instant-gratification, circus-like atmosphere, you can keep it. But when raku is taught seriously, with a respect for its origins and history, it is certainly appropriate for any school situation.

Having said that, as a pottery teaching tool, raku does offer other advantages besides its visual attraction. The relationship between clay and fire is made much more

9–1
Raku is not only exciting for children (and adults!), but it gives them a closer view of what happens during the firing process.

obvious as the students view the pots in the kiln and as they are removed red hot from the chamber. Glazes and how they mature, through sintering, melting, and smoothing out to a fine surface, are brought to life for unmistakable observation. Raku, in shortening the time span between completed claywork and glazed, fired pot, allows the student a tangible comprehension of the pottery process. In this respect, the raku process becomes more than a singular pottery process. It becomes a gateway to pottery-making as a whole.

Assuming that you do not have raku at your school, first and foremost in the way of hurdles will undoubtedly be to explain this whole thing to your principal, department head, or whoever has to give the OK to the flames, smoke, and whatever else you will need permission for. For this I leave you to your own devices! Rest assured, though, that it can be done. When I started teaching in public high school I was raku firing in an electric kiln located in a cramped office-storeroom, lifting the pots and climbing out a window with the pot on my tongs to a barrel in which the kids would throw in the sawdust and cover it. We were in a concrete, recessed window well that measured about 5' × 15' and was below ground level. Smoke would routinely escape into the classrooms above. Without a doubt, not the safest or most tranquil raku environment. The same assistant principal who thought raku was a perfectly fine activity would not allow me to play music in the classroom because I couldn't justify its relevance to the educational process.

Once beyond the preliminaries, I urge you to place the raku technique in a frame of reference with other pottery processes so the students realize that raku is not the only form that pottery takes. Don't let

raku, or any one approach for that matter, run your program. Aesthetically, raku seems to appeal to everyone immediately, often at the expense of an open attitude toward the results obtained through other firing methods. Whether its the spontaneity, metallic effects, ease (when the teacher takes care of the details of course!), or whatever, it doesn't really matter. The point is to stress that raku is one of many pottery processes, and while its aesthetic appeal is captivating, other methods of pottery-making and firing must be experienced and explored as well. Why? Because despite its attraction, raku is still but one of many creative techniques that becomes even more exciting when the knowledge and experience of other pottery processes is brought to it. Explaining this is probably the most difficult task I face each year with my own students at Thayer Academy. Once they do raku, they become addicted. After I go through all of the possible historical, technical, aesthetic, and otherwise scholarly-sounding rhetoric, I almost always have to demand that they fire reduction and oxidation stoneware and porcelain as well. To think that one would need to be coerced into firing reduction stoneware and porcelain!

Most important in preparing for the raku firing is to be sure that you have explained the firing process and that the students know what to expect. Of course, if they have never seen a raku firing before, no matter how much you tell them first, the firing will probably be surprising. In setting up the actual raku firing, you must overcome some serious logistical concerns. As you have seen, a special raku kiln is not a prerequisite for being able to do raku. An everyday electric kiln is perfectly suitable. Much more important is where the kiln is located in relation to the outdoors. Forget about any kind of smoking

9–2
Careful instruction is critical to ensuring a successful and safe workshop.

indoors. If your circumstances require you to fire indoors, you must be close enough to carry your pots outside and reduce there. (See Figs. 4–18, 4–19) The nature of the raku process will be different when using an electric kiln indoors than using a gas kiln outdoors. There is not as much excitement, drama, or involvement by the participants, and you will be limited to one firing a day. In some respects, planning for an indoor firing is more critical, for dropping a pot indoors on a hard floor is potentially more serious than dropping one outdoors. At any rate, whether firing indoors or out, the most important thing is safety. I have had kids as young as eight actually lifting their pots out of the kiln and placing them in the postfiring container. Talk about excitement!

The need for the extreme attention to safety may seem obvious, especially when dealing with very young children or, for that matter, with kids of all ages. How-

ever, don't become complacent or careless in setting up the experience for older students, high school and beyond.

The kiln site must be clean and clear of all extraneous debris. Supervision is essential, and each child must be assigned to a particular task. As the leader and director of the firing, it's impossible to keep an eye on every child, making sure that someone doesn't stray into a hot pot. Simple monitoring of that kind should be done by another person to whom you have already explained the process. Now there are only a limited number of "jobs" to be manned during the firing, and chances are you will have more children than tasks. Let one group participate during one load with another getting their chance during the next load. Limit the movements of the kids to small confined areas. In other words, don't have a child lift a pot and have to carry it around to the other side of the kiln to place it in a container. Have all your containers placed in logical spots and choreograph the whole event. The children lifting pots out of the kiln must know where they are to go with them. As a general rule, the younger the children, the fewer who should be taking part at once. No more than two children (or people of any age for that matter), should be removing pots from the kiln during any one load. If you are having the kids glaze at the same time, locate the glazing and washing areas a good distance from the firing area. Keep your reduction materials stored away from the firing area as well to avoid accidentally igniting it with a hot pot or flying sparks. Ultimately the safety of your participants is your responsibility. You must use your own good judgment, based on your level of experience and expertise, in deciding what kind of situation you are capable of directing.

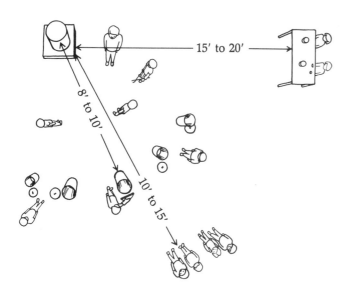

9–3
Be sure to provide plenty of space for movement around the kiln and containers. Spectators should be kept away from the immediate firing area.

An appropriate introduction and closure is important in solidifying the students' understanding and appreciation of the raku technique. Schedule enough time for the students so that they can experience the entire process without having to rush to the next class. If this means a special afterschool time slot, then so be it.

These are just a few of the special considerations regarding the raku technique in school situations. Undoubtedly you will encounter others given your own circumstances. Remember that when the process is presented seriously it can be a most educational and inspirational experience for the students and a rewarding one for you.

9–4
A class of six- to eight-year-olds at The Potters School.

9–5
Children can participate in all phases of the raku process just like adults!

Raku Workshops

So you think you're ready to present the raku process in a workshop setting before an audience of your peers. There are some significant differences between teaching the raku technique in the classroom and presenting a stand-alone workshop. As a teacher in a classroom, your presentation of the raku technique is part of a larger agenda. It will most likely be one topic within a broad curriculum. You meet with your students on a regular basis and have the opportunity and even obligation to understand their perceptions, intentions, and ways they learn most effectively. Conveniently, whether it is the next day, week, or month, you can reiterate a point, elaborate on a particular detail, or correct a mistake *you* may have made. Add to this the fact that your students are probably not about to rush out and do raku on their own, and you have a comfortable, controlled teaching environment without the likelihood of any immediate repercussions.

In addition to being well versed and experienced in all phases of the raku process, in the workshop forum you need to go one step further. Feeling comfortable and confident enough to teach raku in a classroom or doing it on your own is not enough. You have one chance to present yourself and your knowledge, and the information you give is the information that will be used when you are no longer present. You must be more than well versed and knowledgeable—you must be intimately familiar with every detail of the process. My intention is not to scare you away from giving a workshop but rather to remind you that the present and future safety of the students should be first and foremost on your mind. Without that level of comfort, it would be at the least not fair to the participants, and at the worst it could be dangerous.

Having said that, the practical concerns regarding preparation of the kiln site, individual assignments, the gathering of materials, and the other issues discussed above apply here as well. A well-planned workshop is much more than

9–6
There is no substitute for hands-on experience. Monthly raku firings at The Potters School offer instruction in the technique and access to the facilities.

that. In addition, it revolves around fulfilling the needs and expectations of the participants. Will they be experienced potters familiar with general pottery and firing terminology? Will they have done raku before? What do they expect to learn, and through what avenues do you plan on teaching them?

A successful raku workshop or demonstration does not have to be one that traverses the subject from cover to cover. In fact, you are more likely to please the participants and do a more thorough job by restricting the presentation to one or two limited areas, such as the firing process, glazing techniques, kiln building, or traditional raku. Then you can easily set goals for yourself and the workshop and be able to measure the success of your presentation. In short, approach the workshop setting with thorough preparation of its content, materials, and props. Set some educational goals, but be prepared to shift your focus with the leanings of the participants. Under no circumstances should you ever find yourself in an obviously preventable situation such as being out of gas, not have enough reduction containers, or have inappropriate tools or a malfunctioning kiln that cannot be remedied.

Remember that a raku firing whether on your own or with a group is never a completely predictable event. Enjoy the workshop, be prepared to deal with unforeseeable and possibly tricky situations, and take advantage of the opportunity to learn from the combined efforts of those you are teaching and from yourself.

Conclusion

The best conclusion is one that inspires you with some final words of wisdom and causes you to move along enthusiastically with the information and knowledge you have gained here. A kind of "Knute Rockne: Pottery Coach." Since words of wisdom are in short supply these days, the contents of this book will have to suffice!

Above all, raku is a process comprised of many tools; clay, glazes, kiln, and fuel,

Robert Piepenburg. Raku Sculpture. 1990. Poured copper glaze, reduced with sawdust and water-cooled. 34" h. The various sections of this hand-built piece are connected while wet with short sections of 1"-diameter stainless-steel rods. The clay shrinks enough around the rod to make a tight fit, but not enough to crack the clay. Photo: Bill Pelletier.

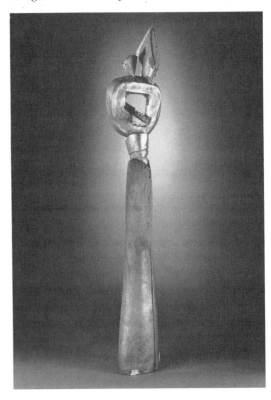

Author. Platter. *1984.*
Wheel-thrown; slip trailed
and splattered glaze. 24" d.
Photo: Robert Arruda.

as well as your own drive, desire, and imagination. Don't let lack of experience or instruction in any aspect of the process hold you back. More often than not, you know more than you think you do, and by feeling free and bold enough to apply this inner knowledge and search out new connections, you can open up a new world.

While there is a greater aesthetic that we are all bound by to a greater or lesser degree, right and wrong and good and bad are measured within the context of the parameters you set up for yourself. It is less important that a particular process or technique works "correctly" by someone else's standards and more important that the result satisfies your expectations. Keep an open mind, allowing and even embracing unexpected results without the

encumbrance of adhering to predetermined formula. Throughout your entire creative involvement, maintain your own aesthetic standards and expectations. It is this dedication to veracity, not compliance with technical matters, that forms the most basic boundary of creativity.

While I have made every attempt to include as much information on the raku process and its variations as possible, I have made no attempt to include every variation, technique, material, or subtlety. That would be an impossible task. Too many deviations, modifications, and individual nuances exist that are limited only by your own vision and your ability to create new connections between techniques and combinations of shared ideas. Use it all and apply it to your work. However, complete the cycle by giving something back, offering some help, some teaching of your own, and return some ideas and your own contributions to the kettle for use by future students of the craft. For there is in fact no conclusion—only beginnings and constant thresholds of departure from the accepted way for you to blaze your own trail of excitement and expression.

Supplies and
Materials

Sources for supplies and materials are often taken for granted by those "in the know." "Oh, expanded metal? Sure, that scrap yard next to the industrial park, where else!" Of course, why didn't I think of that? However, except for obvious ceramics supplies and whatever else may be listed in the catalogue of our local pottery supply, much of the equipment and paraphernalia useful and even critical to the raku potter can be frustrating to locate.

When looking for sources of supplies, start with the Yellow Pages. It's amazing how overlooked this wonderful resource is. Time and again when I suggest that someone look in the Yellow Pages, their reaction is skeptical. Only after they find what they are looking for with a minimum of hassle do they realize how obvious this was. The trick to using the Yellow Pages is to consult the index. If you live in a suburban or rural area with a Yellow Pages the size of your address book, use the index of a Yellow Pages of a nearby, larger city. Then look under that heading in the book for your area.

Always exhaust all local sources for supplies and materials before you search out of your area. Don't assume that because a particular supplier is larger or more well known that it can serve you better than a small local store. Likewise, think beyond the obvious source for a particular item and you may find a wider selection and possibly save some money. For example, compressors and airbrushes can be purchased at pottery suppliers, art supply stores, auto supply stores, paint stores, and automobile painting equipment and supply stores.

Hardware stores interest me, but I do get a variety of reactions from salespeople when in response to, "Can I help you?" I say, "Just looking." Often I will browse the store taking written or mental notes about their inventory. Fasteners, electrical hardware, and all sorts of items designed and sold for one purpose can, with a little imagination, be just the thing you were looking for. The "Grow Thru" product that I found in the landscaping store is a good example. Browsing through a commercial restaurant supplier, I came across large, heavy-duty spatulas perfect for glaze mixing and better than ones sold at a pottery supply for that purpose. There were also inexpensive plastic containers with firm-fitting lids for glaze and slip storage, and large, round stainless-steel bowls that were perfect for draping slabs over and pressing them into. I could go on, but I'm sure you get the idea.

Soluble salts for vapor glazing, fuming, and other techniques discussed can be difficult to locate. Of the pottery suppliers that carry these materials, Standard Ceramic Supply probably has the widest selection. Chemical companies carry them all, but the grades or purity standards of the materials they carry are often much higher and thus more expensive. Don't automatically assume that to be so in all cases, though. For instance, silver nitrate, being a commodity, fluctuates in price. One day I noticed that the price varied from $149.50 to $303.00 per pound for the same grade material! Grades generally range from reagent grade or purer down to technical grade or lower. When calling chemical companies, remember to ask what grade is available. Often chemical companies will sell only to schools or bona fide industries that use chemicals, but this varies also. Order your supplies through a school if you teach or have a friend who teaches. Some companies have technical support services that can be extremely helpful.

Please don't overlook sources of free or almost-free supplies. Among them are lumberyards for sawdust for smoking and scrap wood for wood firing. Also, scrap yards for sheet metal, iron bars, grates, and a variety of exciting items. Check your local plumbing supply or appliance store for refrigerators, freezers, and other junked items that are useful as reduction containers. The point is—be resourceful!

A word about general pottery suppliers. Most pottery supply companies stock a variety of clays, raw materials, firebrick, commercial glazes, underglazes, and so on. They also probably have refractory materials such as fiber and brick and other necessary items such as gloves and tongs. First look to your local or closest pottery supply to see just what items it stocks. If you aren't familiar with one, look in the Yellow Pages or check *Ceramics Monthly*.

Suppliers

Agway Inc., P.O. Box 4571, Syracuse, NY 315–449–7061. Stores throughout the Northeast. All kinds of hardware, farm supplies, and other materials. Various chemicals used on farms. For example, copper sulfate, 5–lb. bag—$7.50!

American Steel and Aluminum, 1080 University Ave., Norwood, MA 02062. 617–762–8014. Expanded metal.

Axner Pottery, P.O. Box 1484, Oviedo, FL 32765. 800–843–7057. Kilns, including raku kilns, tongs, gloves, safety equipment, Mason stains, and more.

Dedell Gas Burner and Equipment Co., R.R. 1 Box 2135, Newfane, VT 05345. 802–365–4575. Complete line of combustion equipment, including specially designed raku burner systems.

Del Amo Chemical Co., 535 W. 152 St., Gardena, CA 90248. 213–532–9214; outside CA., 800–779–2436. Chemicals and supplies, no technical support. Will sell to a registered business of any kind.

Duralight, School St., Riverton, CT 06065. 203–379–3113. Coils for electric kilns. Hundreds are stocked. They can also duplicate your coil if you send the broken pieces. Custom-designed coils as well.

Flinn Scientific Inc., P.O. Box 219, Batavia, IL. 60510. 708–879–6900. Chemicals and supplies. Sells only to science teachers through schools. Their catalog is interesting, with complete data on all chemicals.

Great Lakes Clay and Supply Company, 10 W. Main St., Carpentersville, IL 60110. 708–551–1070. Tongs, gloves, chemicals, burners, refractory supplies, and other general supplies and equipment.

Johnson Gas Appliance Company, 520 E. Ave. N.W., Cedar Rapids, Iowa 52045. 319–365–5267. Burners and burner systems.

Kemper Mfg. Co., 13595 12 St., Chino CA 91710. Tongs sold through distributors.

Kent Pottery Tools Ltd., Pearsons Green, Brenchley, Tonbridge, Kent, England TN 127

DE. Handmade raku tongs and bamboo tools.

Magid Glove and Safety Mfg. Co., 2060 N. Kolmar Ave., Chicago, IL 60639. 800–444–8010. Kevlar gloves, goggles, masks, respirators, and other safety equipment. Very knowledgeable and helpful technical department.

McEnglevan, P.O. Box 31, Danville, IL. 61834. 217–446–0941. Call for local distributor. Foundry supplies, including tongs.

McMaster-Carr Supply Co., P.O. Box 440, New Brunswick, NJ 08903. 201–329–3200. Plants also in Atlanta, Chicago, and Los Angeles. This catalog epitomizes the expression "If we don't have it, you don't need it." In one word: unbelievable! Almost 2,500 pages of absolutely everything—tongs, expanded metal, barrels, tools, sandblasters, gloves, sprayers, refractory cements. There are things here that don't even have uses yet! You must get this catalog.

Miami Cork And Supply, 10160 N.W. 47 St., Sunrise, FL 33351. 800–780–2675. Fiber-lined raku kilns, tongs, and other general supplies.

Nilfisk of America, 224 Great Valley Parkway, Malvern, PA 19355. 215–647–6420. The premier industrial vacuum cleaner. Suitable for fine clay dusts. Sold through distributors but will also sell direct, often at a better price.

Olympic Kilns, 6301 Button Gwinnett Dr., Atlanta, GA 30340. 404–441–5550. Gas and electric kilns, including a gas raku kiln. Sold through distributors.

Peoples Coal and Wood, 55 Mill St., Cumberland, RI 02864. 508–761–6929. Hardwood charcoal and hardwood briquettes.

Pulmosan Protective Equipment, P.O. Box 622, Reading, PA 19603. 800–345–3479. Kevlar gloves, respirators, and goggles. Sells only through distributors but will give you the names of dealers closest to you.

Sara Glove Company, P.O. Box 1940, Waterbury, CT 06722. 800–243–3570. Kevlar gloves, face masks, goggles, and other safety equipment.

Spectrum Chemical, 14422 S. San Pedro St., Gardena, CA 18293. 800–772–8786. Chemicals of all kinds.

Standard Ceramic Supply, P.O. Box 4435, Pittsburgh, PA 15205. 412–276–6333. One of the most complete stocks of raw materials around, including metallic salts, underglazes, glazes, and stains. Also gloves, brick, and other supplies.

Summit Gas Kilns, 2256 Hopson Rd., Land O Lakes, FL 34639. 813–996–2575. A line of top-loading updraft kilns all suitable for raku.

Tri-Ess Sciences Incorporated, 1020 W. Chestnut St., Burbank, CA 91506. 818–247–6910. Chemicals of all kinds, including metallic salts. Variety of other scientific supplies. Interesting catalog.

Westwood Ceramic Supply, 14400 Lomitas Ave., City of Industry, CA 91746. 818–330–0631. A good selection of raw materials, commercial glazes, stains, gloves, and refractory materials.

W. W. Grainger, Inc., 5959 W. Howard St., Chicago, IL 60648. Branches nationwide. A veritable treasure chest of "stuff," including exhaust fans, barrels, electrical, shelving, and hundreds of other items. No craftsperson should be without this catalogue.

Books

The Potters Shop, 31 Thorpe Road, Needham, MA 02194. 617–449–7687. *The* source for books on pottery. Unbelievable selection and service. Special orders also.

Kinokuniya Book Store, 10 West 49 St., New York, NY 10020. 212–765–1461. Also 1581 Webster St., San Francisco, CA 94115. 415–567–7625. Books exclusively on Japan in all subjects. Japanese and English language.

Other Supplies and Equipment

Bricks and refractory supplies. In addition to pottery suppliers, look under bricks and refractories in the Yellow Pages.

Expanded metal. Metal scrap yards, junkyards, steel and aluminum suppliers.

Gas supply, hoses, fittings, tanks. Look under propane or gas companies in the Yellow Pages. Also plumbing suppliers. 20-pound tanks are available in hardware stores, supermarkets, and home centers.

Gloves, Protective equipment, sparkers. Look for welders supplies in the Yellow Pages.

Reduction containers. Hardware stores, industrial cleaning suppliers, janitorial suppliers, farm suppliers, such as Agway in the Northeast. Look in the Yellow Pages under ''Barrels.''

Tongs. Fireplace shops, blacksmith suppliers, foundry suppliers.

Wire mesh, hardware cloth. Hardware stores, building materials suppliers, farm supply stores.

U.K. Equivalents for North American Materials

The following substitutions are suggested by *The Potters Complete Book of Clay and Glazes* (see bibliography). They are based on chemical analysis and should be employed on a direct substitution basis. Slight differences in results, as compared to using the listed ingredients, may occur but should pose no problems. When in doubt as to a suitable substitute, consult your clay materials supplier, who should have on hand analysis charts and the knowledge to offer logical suggestions. The U.K. manufacturers listed are: **P&S**—Podmore & Sons; **P**—Potclays Ltd.; **WBB**—Watts Blake Bearne & Co.; **HM**—Harrison Mayer Ltd.; and **W**—Wengers Ltd.

Listed Material	*U.K. Equivalent*
AP Green Fireclay	Glenboig Fireclay
Cedar Heights Goldart	**WBB** Super Strength NDK
Tennessee Ball Clay	**HM** Blue Ball Clay; **WBB** TWVD Ball Clay; **W** Ball Clay #1
Custer Feldspar	**P&S** Potash Feldspar; **W** Potash Feldspar
Missouri Fireclay	Any good quality fireclay
OM4 Ball Clay	Most any ball clay
PBX Fireclay	**P** Fireclay #6
Redart	Etruria Marl
Macaloid	Suspension agent similar in use to Bentonite; a plasticizer when used in clay bodies. Formula: Li_2O, MgO, SiO_2
Frit 3134	A borosilicate frit that melts at cone 06. Substitutes: Hommel #14 or #242; Pemco #54
Frit 3304	A lead frit used in glazes in the 08-02 range, where lead is necessary to achieve certain colors
Superpax	Any commercial opacifier
EPK	**P&S** China Clay; **P** China Clay

Note: Mason stains are commercially prepared ceramic colors supplied in dry powder form.

Bibliography and Suggested Reading

The following is not an all-encompassing bibliography of books on pottery and ceramics. Nor does it include every book that whispers raku somewhere within its covers. It is a selective one, comprised of those books and articles that I used in my research plus those that will complement one's study of raku. Included are books on raku specifically, as well as glaze recipe books, technical titles, and books on health and safety and on other related pottery processes. I have also included a list of well-written general handbooks for the beginning potter, including some on throwing and handbuilding. All the books should be available at major public and university libraries. I have indicated with codes books that are out of print or those that may be otherwise difficult to obtain.

Theoretically, any bookstore can obtain any book for you if it is in print. In practice, though, special orders can take weeks or months. The best source for books on pottery and ceramics is *The Potters Shop*. Many pottery suppliers also carry books.

OP—out of print
FP—foreign publisher, difficult to obtain in the United States.

General Pottery Handbooks

Many, if not most, general pottery handbooks contain some information on raku. It may be a brief reference, some recipes, or even a full-fledged section on the subject. An asterisk (*) indicates books that include substantial information on the raku technique.

Birks, Tony. *Pottery: A Complete Guide to Pottery-Making Techniques.** Asheville: Lark Books; London: Alphabooks/A & C Black, 1988.

Casson, Michael. *The Craft of the Potter.* New York: Barron's Educational Series, 1979.

Clark, Kenneth. *A Potter's Manual.* Secaucus, NJ: Chartwell Books 1987.

Conrad, John. *Contemporary Ceramic Techniques.** Englewood Cliffs, NJ: Prentice-Hall, 1979. OP

Harvey, David. *Imaginative Pottery.** London: A & C Black, 1983.

Leach, Bernard. *A Potter's Book.** London: Faber and Faber, 1946.

Nelson, Glen C. *Ceramics: A Potters Handbook,* 5th edition. New York: Holt, Rinehart and Winston, 1984.

Nigrosh, Leon. *Claywork.** Worcester: Davis Publications, 1986.

Speight, Charlotte. *Hands in Clay.** Mountain View: Mayfield Publishing Co., 1989.

Technical/Kilns/Recipes/Ceramic Science

Brodie, Regis C. *The Energy-Efficient Potter.* New York: Watson-Guptill, 1982.

Brody, Harvey. *The Book of Low-Fire Ceramics.** New York: Holt, Rinehart and Winston, 1980. OP

Cardew, Michael. *Pioneer Pottery.* New York: St. Martins Press, 1969. OP

Chappell, James. *The Potters Complete Book of Clay and Glazes.* New York: Watson-Guptill. 1977. Rev. ed., 1991.

Colson, Frank. *Kiln Building with Space-Age Materials.** Englewood Cliffs, NJ: Prentice-Hall, 1975. OP

Conrad, John. *Advanced Ceramic Manual.* San Diego: Falcon Publishers, 1988.

———. *Ceramic Formulas: The Complete Compendium.* San Diego: Falcon Publishers, 1989.

———. *Contemporary Ceramic Formulas.* New York: Macmillan, 1980.

——— *Studio Pottery Dictionary.* San Diego: Falcon Publishers, 1990.

Cooper, Emmanuel. *Coopers Book Of Glaze Recipes.* London: Batsford. 1987 FP

———. *Potters Book of Glaze Recipes.* London: Batsford, 1980. FP

Davis, Harry. *The Potters Alternative.* Radnor: Chilton Book Co., 1989.

Fraser, Harry. *Ceramic Faults and Their Remedies.* London: A & C Black, 1986. FP

Gibson, John. *Contemporary Pottery Decoration.* Radnor: Chilton Book Co.; London: A & C Black, 1987.

Gregory, Ian. *Kiln Building.* London: A & C Black, 1977. OP

Hamer, Frank. *The Potters Dictionary of Materials and Techniques.* London: A & C Black, 1975. FP

Hopper, Robin. *Ceramic Spectrum.* Radnor: Chilton Book Co. 1984.

Memmott, Harry. *Artists Guide to the Use of Ceramic Oxides.* Burwood, Australia: Victoria College Press, 1986. FP

Nigrosh, Leon. *Low Fire, Other Ways to Work in Clay.** Worcester: Davis Publications, 1980.

Olsen, Frederick L. *The Kiln Book.* Radnor: Chilton Book Co.; London: A & C Black, 1983.

Parks, Dennis. *Potters Guide to Raw Glazing and Oil Firing.* London: A & C Black, 1980 FP

Parmelee, Cullen. *Ceramic Glazes.* Boston: Cahners Publishing Co., 1951. OP

Rhodes, Daniel. *Clay and Glazes for the Potter,* revised edition. Radnor: Chilton Book Co.; London: A & C Black, 1973.

———. *Kilns: Design, Construction, and Operation,* 2d edition. Radnor: Chilton Book Co., 1981.

Riegger, Hal. *Primitive Pottery.* New York: Van Nostrand Reinhold, 1972. OP

Sanders, Herbert. *Glazes for Special Effects.** New York: Watson-Guptill, 1974. OP

Staples, Ron. *Air Brushing Guide for Ceramics.* Franklin Park: Badger Air Brush Co., 1984.

Starkey, Peter. *Saltglaze.* London: A & C Black, 1977. OP

Sutherland, Brian. *Glazes from Natural Sources.* London: Batsford, 1987. FP

Tichane, Robert. *Clay Bodies.* Painted Post: New York Glaze Institute, 1990. Available only direct from the publisher.

Wechsler, Susan. *Low-Fire Ceramics.** New York: Watson-Guptill, 1981. OP

Williams, Gerry, et al. *Studio Potter Book.** New York: Van Nostrand Reinhold, 1979. OP

Raku

Dickerson, John. *Raku Handbook.* New York: Van Nostrand Reinhold, 1974. OP

Hirsch, Rick, and Christopher Tyler. *Raku.* New York: Watson-Guptill, 1975. OP

Lynggaard, Finn. *Pottery: Raku Technique.* New York: Van Nostrand Reinhold, 1970. OP

Piepenburg, Robert. *Raku Pottery.* New York: Macmillan, 1972. Rev. ed., Ann Arbor: Pebble Press, 1991.

Riegger, Hal. *Raku Art and Technique.* New York: Macmillan, 1970. OP

Romberg, James. *Ceramics Today, James M. Romberg.* Geneva: Editions Olizane, 1983. OP

Health and Safety

Clark, Nancy. *Ventilation: A Practical Guide for Artists, Craftspeople, and Others in the Arts.* New York: Nick Lyons Books, 1984.

McCann, Michael. *Artist Beware.* New York: Watson-Guptill, 1979.

———. *Health Hazards Manual for the Artist,* 3d edition. New York: Nick Lyons Books, 1985.

Qualley, Charles. *Safety in the Art Room.* Worcester: Davis Publications, 1986.

Hand-Building and Throwing for Beginners

Blandino, Betty. *Coiled Pottery.* Radnor: Chilton Book Co.; London: A & C Black, 1984.

Campbell, Donald. *Using the Potters Wheel.* Englewood Cliffs, NJ: Prentice-Hall, 1978.

Colbeck, John. *Pottery: The Technique of Throwing.* New York: Watson-Guptill, 1988.

Sapiro. *Clay: Handbuilding.* Worcester: Davis Publications, nd.

———. *Clay: The Potters Wheel.* Worcester: Davis Publications, nd.

Woody, Elspeth. *Handbuilding Ceramic Forms.* New York: Farrar, Straus and Giroux, 1978. OP

———. *Pottery on the Wheel.* New York: Farrar, Straus and Giroux, 1975. OP

Other Related Titles

Berensohn, Paulus. *Finding One's Way with Clay.* New York: Simon and Schuster, 1972. OP

Fujioka, Ryoichi. *Tea Ceremony Utensils.* New York: Weatherhill, 1973. OP

Henri, Robert. *The Art Spirit.* Philadelphia: J. B. Lippincott, 1960.

Koyama, Fujio. *The Heritage of Japanese Ceramics.* New York: Weatherhill, 1973. OP

Okakura, Kakuzo. *The Book of Tea.* Rutland, VT: Charles Tuttle, 1956.

Piccolpasso, Cipriano. *The Three Books of the Potters Art.* Translation and notes by Ronald Lightbrown and Alan Caiger-Smith. London: Scolar Press, 1980. FP

Rawson, Philip. *Ceramics.* London: Oxford University Press, 1971.

Richards, M. C. *Centering in Pottery, Poetry, and the Person.* Middletown, CT: Wesleyan University Press, 1962.

Sanders, Herbert. *The World of Japanese Ceramics.* Palo Alto, CA: Kodansha, 1967. OP

Sadler, A. L. *Cha-No-Yu: The Japanese Tea Ceremony.* Rutland, VT: Charles Tuttle, 1962.

Sen, Soshitsu. *Chado: The Japanese Way of Tea.* New York: Weatherhill, 1979.

———. ed. *Chanoyu: The Urasanke Tradition of Tea.* New York: Weatherhill, 1988.

Tanaka, Sen' O. *The Tea Ceremony.* New York: Kodansha, 1973. OP

Troy, Jack. *Salt-Glazed Ceramics.* New York: Watson-Guptill, 1977. OP

Yanagi, Soetsu. *Unknown Craftsman.* Palo Alto, CA: Kodansha, 1972.

Articles

Behrens, Richard. *"Vapor Glazing in a Saggar."* Ceramics Monthly 24:6 (June 1976).

Brisson, Harriet. *"Sawdust Firing."* Ceramics Monthly 24:8 (October 1976).

Clarke, R. Bede. *"Low-Temperature Salt/Saggar Firing."* Ceramics Monthly 36:9 (November 1988).

Davis, James C. *"Cracking Raku Glazes with Oil Reduction."* Ceramics Monthly 22:1 (January 1974).

Dunham, Judith. *"Paul Soldner."* American Craft 42:5 (October–November 1985).

Gibbs, Peter. *"Salt Pit and Sawdust Firing."* Ceramics Monthly 35:2 (February 1987).

Gilbertson, Warren. *"Making of Raku Ware and Its Value in the Teaching of Beginner's Pottery in America." Bulletin of the American Ceramic Society.* 22 (February 1943).

Hindes, Chuck. *"Saggar Firing." Studio Potter* 7:2

Lehman, Dick. *"Planning a Potter's Sabbatical." Ceramics Monthly* 37:6 (Summer 1989).

Liskey, Ronda. *"A Production Raku Kiln." Ceramics Monthly* 37:9 (November 1989).

Moomey, Diane. *"Low-Fire Surface Effects." Ceramics Monthly* 32:5 (May 1984).

Riegger, Hal. *"Raku." Ceramics Monthly* 7:6 (June 1959).

Soldner, Paul. *"The American Way of Raku." Ceramic Review* 124 (July–August 1990).

———. *"Keynote Address," National Potters Conference, Adelaide, Australia." Pottery in Australia* 22:2 (November–December 1983).

Spangler, Glenn. *"Smoke and Color." Ceramics Monthly* 34:6 (Summer 1986).

Troy, Jack. *"Fuming in the Salt Kiln." Craft Horizons* 32:3 (June 1972).

Wilson, Lana. *"Charcoal and Metallic Salts." Ceramics Monthly* 35:8 (October 1987).

Videos

Videos are all VHS.

Jim Romberg, Raku Ceramics. Ashland: Ashland Video Productions. 1990.

Paul Soldner, Thoughts on Creativity. American Ceramics Society. 1989.

Piepenburg on Raku, Clay, Glazes, and Tongs. Ann Arbor: Robert Piepenburg, 1989.

Piepenburg on Kiln Building.

Piepenburg on Firing and Reduction.

Piepenburg on Smoke Firing.

Pottery Magazines

American Ceramics, 9 E. 45 St., New York, NY 10017.

Ceramic Review. 21 Carnaby St., London, W1V 1PH, England.

Ceramics Monthly. Box 12448, Columbus, Ohio 43212.

Pottery in Australia. 48 Burton St., Darlinghurst, NSW 2010, Australia.

Studio Potter. Box 65, Goffstown, NH 03045.

New Zealand Potter. P.O. Box 881, Auckland, New Zealand.

Index